After the Earth Summit:
The Future of Environmental Governance

Hilary F. French

Erik Hagerman and Megan Ryan, Research Assistants
Sandra Postel, Vice President for Research

Ed Ayres, Editor

Worldwatch Paper 107
March 1992

© Worldwatch Institute, 1992
Library of Congress Catalog Number 92-080516
ISBN 1-878071-08-4

Printed on recycled paper

Table of Contents

Introduction

On April 28, 1986, the office of Soviet Foreign Minister Eduard Shevardnadze received an avalanche of inquiries from foreign governments demanding an explanation for the high levels of radioactivity suddenly being detected over their territories. "That was the day of Chernobyl," recalled Shevardnadze several years later. "Even before we pronounced this name and even before we revealed for ourselves and the whole world the scope of the catastrophe which it designated, it had already become abundantly clear that from then on, no ecological calamity could any longer be regarded as pertaining solely to that national territory on which it had occurred." Subsequent events added poignant emphasis to this statement. A year later, the Soviet Union was dissolved—but left behind it a crippled Chernobyl that may pose dangers to the newly independent republics and their neighbors for decades or even centuries to come.[1]

As Shevardnadze's experience indicates, environmental problems not only cross borders with impunity, but challenge long-cherished tenets of international relations—particularly the assumption that nations have complete dominion over matters within their boundaries. With increasing frequency, Chernobyl-like events—large and small—have entangled whole regions, and sometimes the whole world, in problems that no individual nation can solve. In the same year as the Chernobyl nuclear reactor explosion, an enormous spill of dyes, insecticides, and mercury caused by a fire at a Basel, Switzerland warehouse killed fish and other aquatic life along 300 kilometers of the Rhine river, which courses through four countries. Around the same time, massive quantities of hazardous waste were being hauled from Europe to the Nigerian fishing village of Koko, where an Italian waste broker had successfully bribed unwitting villagers into accepting it. Some 8,000 drums of the deadly stuff were found in an open field, with children playing among them.[2]

I would like to thank Erik Hagerman and Megan Ryan for their help with research and Elizabeth P. Barratt-Brown, Jeffrey Dunoff, Lee A. Kimball, William R. Pace, Gareth Porter, Philippe Sands, Frederik van Bolhuis, Miranda S. Wecker, Durwood Zaelke, and my colleagues at the Worldwatch Institute for their comments on preliminary drafts of this paper.

6 Such incidents illustrate how easily environmental threats now violate boundaries—whether by air, water, or human transport. Wind currents, rain patterns, rivers, and streams carry pollutants hundreds or even thousands of kilometers from their sources. Some 200 river basins are shared by two or more countries. On an even larger scale, the global environmental problems of ozone depletion, climate change, deforestation, and the loss of the earth's biological diversity threaten all nations. Any one country acting alone is powerless in the face of these problems.[3]

National sovereignty—the power of a country to control events within its territory—has lost much of its meaning in today's world, where borders are routinely breached by pollution, international trade, financial flows, and refugees. Increasingly, they may be eroded by such forces as climatic warming, migrations, and the depletion of the earth's ozone shield. Because all of these forces can affect environmental trends, international treaties and institutions are proving ever more critical to addressing ecological threats. Nations are in effect ceding portions of their sovereignty to the international community, and beginning to create a new system of international environmental governance as a means of solving otherwise-unmanageable problems.[4]

International efforts to protect the natural environment date at least to the 1870s, when Switzerland tried to establish a regional agreement to protect the nesting sites of migratory birds. But the move to internationalize environmental policymaking did not gain serious momentum until the 1970s. To date, governments have adopted more than 170 environmental treaties concerning subjects of shared concern: acid rain, ocean pollution, endangered species protection, hazardous wastes export, and the preservation of Antarctica, as well as ozone depletion. More than two-thirds of these agreements have been reached since the landmark U.N. Conference on the Human Environment was held in Stockholm in 1972. Governments have also deployed international institutions such as the United Nations Environment Programme (UNEP), created at the Stockholm conference, to negotiate treaties and help make them work.[5]

Ecological issues have in the space of a few years become a central feature of international relations. In the late eighties, when global warming first emerged as a pressing international priority, Gro Harlem Bruntland, Mikhail Gorbachev, Margaret Thatcher, and other world leaders seemed at times to be competing to be the greenest actors on the world stage. At the 1989 G-7 summit meeting, environmental questions dominated the discussions and the communiqué.[6]

In recent years, however, rhetoric about the need for international environmental governance has far outweighed effective action. In the year preceding the June, 1992 United Nations Conference on Environment and Development (UNCED), it became clear that this so-called "Earth Summit" would be a critical test of resolve for world leaders. The agenda for the Rio meeting promised historic breakthroughs: treaties covering global warming and the loss of biodiversity; an action plan covering oceans, forests, toxic chemicals, and other issues; and an "Earth Charter" to lay down a set of basic international environmental principles. But it was also clear that such far-reaching agreements and resolutions would not yield progress unless the participating governments could find adequate ways to implement and pay for them.[7]

The current system of environmental treaties falls short on several counts. Existing treaties and agreements are often weak and unenforceable. For some critical environmental threats, such as greenhouse warming and biodiversity loss, no treaty yet exists at all. And governments have not yet ceded to international organizations either the powers or the financial resources they will need to stave off ecological disaster. Most of today's international institutions were fashioned in the forties and fifties, when environmental issues were not yet even on national agendas. Fundamental reforms will be needed if yesterday's institutions are to respond to today's—and tomorrow's— challenges.

What will be the shape of these institutions in the post-UNCED era? Most observers agree that the tasks delegated to international institutions by governments are best limited to those that require international cooperation for resolution. Explained Maurice Strong, Secretary-General of UNCED, in a 1987 speech: "The prime organizing principle for any system of governance should be that responsibility for every activity should be vested in the level closest to the people affected at which it can be managed most effectively." Under this dictum, local and national governments would retain control over their own affairs wherever possible. Regional agreements and institutions such as the European Community's environmental arm and the Central American

8 Commission on Environment and Development will grow in numbers and in strength. Only those issues requiring truly global governance, such as ozone depletion and global warming, will need to be dealt with at that level.[8]

In addition to protecting the prerogatives of local or regional governments wherever possible, international environmental governance will need to protect the interests of the developing world, in which perceived priorities are different from those of the dominant industrial nations. During the months preceding the UNCED conference, there were disturbing signs that these divergent perceptions were creating new antagonisms. To resolve these, the international environmental agenda needs to be linked with the broader economic and development context of which it is a part. Encouraging full developing-country participation in international environmental governance will require more debt relief, reduction of trade barriers, and short-term aid for the hungry or poor. Without these measures, developing countries may be unable to focus on meeting their longer-term environmental commitments.[9]

International institutional development is not keeping pace with either the world's ever-growing interdependence or the rapidly deteriorating condition of the Earth. Existing treaties and declarations represent embryonic attempts to set the world on a sustainable course, and indeed they have led to some important gains. (See Table 1.) But in the long run, to achieve only modest success in this realm will not be enough. Real success in reversing environmental decline will not be possible until more fundamental changes are wrought in the mechanisms of governance themselves.[10]

Preserving a Common Heritage

In his seminal 1968 essay, "The Tragedy of the Commons," ecologist Garrett Hardin compared today's predicament with the degradation of medieval common grazing lands. He described how individual cowherders pursued short-term economic gains to the detriment of everyone's long-term future, knowing that one individual's efforts to conserve the resource base would be overwhelmed by the actions of others. Concluded Hardin: "Ruin is the destination toward which all men rush,

"Environmental governance as presently constituted
is having effect—but not enough effect,
and not nearly fast enough."

each pursuing his interest in a society which believes in the freedom of the commons. Freedom in a commons brings ruin to us all."[11]

9

In the quarter-century since Hardin issued his lament, the world community has begun to take its implications to heart. Treaties have been devised to protect numerous "commons," with special attention to five large categories that require particularly strong international cooperation: the atmosphere, the oceans and seas, the biological diversity of the earth, the continent of Antarctica, and the global economy—which, though not a commons in the conventional sense of the term, also functions as one in the way it helps to transport environmental problems around the world. For each of these commons, a summary of what has been achieved—and what has not—will provide clues to the kinds of fundamental changes needed in environmental governance to avert what Hardin called "ruin" on a global scale.

The most universal "commons" is the atmosphere. International agreements have slowed the damage from acid rain in Europe, and will slow the thinning of the ozone shield worldwide, thereby preventing millions of cancer deaths. But no agreements have been reached on the even larger threat of global warming, despite disturbing suggestions that the warming may have begun. Governance as presently constituted is having effect—but not enough effect, and not nearly fast enough.[12]

One of the first real successes in environmental governance has been Europe's effort to combat transboundary air pollution and acid rain. In the seventies, scientists discovered that automotive, industrial, and power plant pollutants that could be transported long distances were acidifying lakes and damaging forests and crops. Under the auspices of the U.N.'s Economic Commission for Europe (ECE), 33 countries in Europe and North America signed a treaty in 1979, the Convention on Long-Range Transboundary Air Pollution, that committed them to conduct joint research and monitoring on the problem. It also set in motion negotiations to reduce emissions of sulfur dioxide (SO_2) and volatile organic compounds on a specific schedule and to stabilize nitrogen oxides (NO_x) discharges. By now, most ECE countries have signed these agreements and several have made commitments to go beyond them. It is also noteworthy that several countries still have *not* agreed to reduce their emissions—and the damage done by acid rain and pollution in the

Table 1. International Environmental Governance:
Some Notable Accomplishments—and Remaining Challenges[1]

Issue	Accomplishment[1]	Remaining Challenge
Acid Rain in Europe	Sulfur dioxide emissions (a cause of acid rain) have fallen dramatically in Western Europe from 1980-1990 (Austria by 75%, Belgium by 49%) under a 1979 treaty on transboundary air pollution and subsequent tightening measures.	Cuts not great enough to adequately protect ecosystems. Damage to plant and aquatic life continues.
Depletion of Stratospheric Ozone	Global consumption of CFCs (a principal cause of ozone depletion) has decreased from a peak of 1.2 billion kg in 1987 to an estimated 682 million kg in 1991.	Ozone depletion is proceeding twice as fast as expected over parts of the northern hemisphere and 200,000 additional deaths from skin cancer in the U.S. alone could occur during the next 50 years as a result.
Nuclear Weapons Testing	The health threat of radiation from atmospheric testing has decreased markedly since the 1963 limited nuclear weapons test ban. In Moscow, beta radiation levels fell from a maximum daily average of 26.6 millicures/km^2 in 1962 to 0.34 in 1988.	Underground nuclear testing, not covered by the ban, has continued over the past two decades, producing significant localized radioactive pollution.
Mediterranean Sea	About 80% of all Mediterranean beaches offered "clean and safe" bathing in 1988, up from 65% when the Mediterranean Action Plan was launched in 1975.	Some 650,000 tons of petroleum and other hydrocarbons are released into the Mediterranean each year (17 times the amount of oil leaked from the Exxon Valdez off the coast of Alaska); pollution from agricultural runoff is a serious problem.

Whaling	The worldwide whale kill has dropped dramatically over the past decades under tightening International Whaling Commission (IWC) quotas, culminating with a ban on commercial whaling effective as of 1986. Whale harvests fell from 38,977 in 1970 to 688 in 1990[2].	Iceland has announced its intention to withdraw from the IWC effective June 30, 1992. Much of the whaling ostensibly conducted for research purposes, still permitted despite the commercial whaling ban, has been for projects of questionable scientific merit.
Ivory Trade	Within months of the 1990 ban on commercial trade in elephant ivory, the bottom dropped out of the world ivory market and poaching, which had killed 70,000 elephants a year, fell by 80% in most of Africa. Poaching incidents in Kenya decreased from 1,500 in 1989 to 30 in 1990.	South Africa, Zimbabwe, Botswana, Namibia, and Malawi are lobbying to have the ban lifted for their territories. This could cause increases in poaching elsewhere in Africa as well, since illegal ivory could potentially be shipped through those countries for which the ban is lifted.
Preservation of Antarctica	Antarctica is protected from mining, military activities, nuclear tests and radioactive waste imports under the Antarctic Treaty System. Mining exploration and development are banned for the next 50 years under a 1991 agreement.	Pollution caused by tourism and scientific research could alter the continent's pristine environment. There continues to be friction over the harvesting of marine life, most notably krill.
International Hazardous Waste Trade	A large portion of the world has been closed off to the hazardous waste trade. Hazardous waste imports by 69 former European colonies have fallen under the Lomé Agreement.	The bulk of hazardous waste imports has shifted from Africa to the Caribbean, South and Central America, and Asia. Illegal activities persist and countries seek loopholes so that the trade can continue.

[1] Each of the listed accomplishments resulted at least partly from an international agreement. However, the impacts of international and domestic policies cannot be entirely separated, and are often mutually reinforcing.
[2] The 688 figure is attributable to aboriginal hunting quotas and harvests for scientific research that are still permitted by the IWC.

Source: Worldwatch Institute, based on sources documented in endnote 10.

mean time has been extensive. It is likely that the SO_2 and NO_x agreements themselves will soon be revised to call for deeper cuts.[13]

While environmentalists argue that the reduction commitments are not yet steep enough to adequately protect ecosystems, they are far better than nothing. Emissions data suggest that a few countries may not meet the targets on time, but overall progress toward meeting the stated goals has been impressive. (See Table 2.) As a result of commitments made through the ECE talks, as well as of similar legislation passed by the European Community, governments have passed national laws spurring private actions. Scrubbers have been added to power plants in Germany, and catalytic converters are being required on automobiles throughout Western Europe. The countries lagging most in meeting their goals are in Eastern Europe, where hard currency to purchase the needed technologies has been scarce.

In the governance of the atmosphere, the greatest success story to date has been the effort to protect the ozone layer. In the early eighties, governments were confronted with mounting evidence that the ozone layer— which protects the earth from ultraviolet radiation that can cause skin cancer, lower agricultural yields, and damage marine life—was being depleted by chemical reactions high in the atmosphere. The offending compounds were chlorine- and bromine-containing industrial chemicals such as chlorofluorocarbons (CFCs) and halons. In September 1987, negotiators signed an historic agreement—the Montreal Protocol on Substances that Deplete the Ozone Layer—which called for emissions of CFCs in industrial countries to be cut in half by 1998, and for emissions of halons to be frozen at 1986 levels by 1992. The U.S. Environmental Protection Agency (EPA) estimated that these reductions would prevent millions of cases of cataracts and potentially fatal skin cancers worldwide.[14]

A few years later, new evidence emerged that the ozone layer was disappearing far more rapidly than the negotiators had thought. The parties to the protocol quickly returned to the negotiating table. After a series of meetings, 93 nations agreed in June 1990 to stop using CFCs altogether by 2000 and to extend the treaty's provisions to several previously unregulated ozone-depleting chemicals. Developing countries, led by India and China, argued forcefully that it was unfair of industrial coun-

Table 2: Commitments to Reduce Sulfur Dioxide Emissions in Europe

Country	1980 Emissions	1990[1] Emissions	Reductions Achieved (1980-1990)	Total Reductions Promised[2]
	(thousand tons)		(percent)	(percent)
Austria	370	94	–75	–70 by 1995
Belgium	828	420	–49	–50 by 1995
Bulgaria	1,034	1,030	0	–30 by 1993
Czechoslovakia	3,100	2,800	–10	–30 by 1993
Denmark	448	266	–41	–50 by 1995
France	3,338	1,334	–60	–50 by 1990
West Germany[3]	3,210	1,060	–67	–65 by 1993
Hungary	1,632	1,164	–29	–30 by 1993
Italy	3,800	2,410	–37	–30 by 1993
Netherlands	466	254	–45	–50 by 1995
Norway	142	60	–58	–50 by 1994
Poland	4,100	4,500	+10	—
Spain	3,250	2,190	–33	—
Sweden	514	204	–60	–68 by 1995
Soviet Union[4]	12,800	9,580	–25	–30 by 1993
United Kingdom	4,848	3,832	–21	–30 by 1999
Yugoslavia	1,300	1,550	+19	—

[1]Except where otherwise noted, figures are preliminary 1990 data. In other cases, it is the most recent data officially submitted to the Co-operative Programme for Monitoring an Evaluation of the Long-range Transmission of Air Pollutants in Europe (EMEP). For France, Germany, the Netherlands, Norway, and Yugoslavia, this is 1989 data; for Czechoslovakia, 1988; for Italy, 1987; and for Spain, 1985.
[2]Under the 1985 sulfur dioxide protocol, signatories agreed to reduce their emissions by 30 percent of 1980 levels by 1993.
[3]This commitment was made before the unification of Germany.
[4]European part of the Soviet Union. This commitment was made before the Republics gained independence and the country ceased to exist.

Sources: Emissions data from Trond Iversen et al., *Calculated Budgets for Airborne Acidifying Components in Europe, 1985, 1987, 1988, 1989 and 1990*, Technical Report No. 91 (Trondheim, Norway: Det Norske Meteorologiske Institutt, August 1991), for EMEP, U.N. Economic Commission for Europe, Geneva. National targets from "Emissions are falling...but is it enough?," *Acid Magazine*, September 8, 1989.

tries to expect the Third World to incur the costs of switching to CFC substitutes to solve a problem they had little role in creating. After intensive bargaining and a last-minute policy reversal by the United States, participants agreed to establish a fund of up to $240 million to help developing countries purchase CFC substitutes.[15]

By the usual standards of international diplomacy, the ozone negotiations were remarkably rapid. In little more than two years, the world community had moved from a broad statement of concern about the problem—but with no agreement on what to do about it—to a system of international regulation that would affect powerful commercial interests and products widely used in everyday life. Within another three years, governments had recognized the shortcomings of the original document and substantially revised it.[16]

But the rapid accumulation of data even since the 1990 agreement underscores the fact that the job is not yet done. New findings by the U.S. National Aeronautics and Space Administration (NASA) released in April, 1991 showed depletion proceeding twice as fast as expected over parts of the northern hemisphere—and suggested that 200,000 additional deaths from skin cancer in the United States alone could occur during the next fifty years as a result. Still more alarming news appeared in February, 1992, when NASA reported finding chlorine over New England and eastern Canada at a level fifty percent greater than any previously seen over Antarctica—site of the ozone hole. The new data has spurred a call to revise the treaty once more. Possible steps include accelerating the phaseout of CFCs and more tightly controlling some of the proposed CFC substitutes that, though less damaging, have themselves been identified as ozone depleters.[17]

The international community is now putting the ozone experience to use in its effort to address what is perhaps the ultimate atmospheric threat—global warming. Most scientists believe that carbon dioxide (released from fossil fuel burning and deforestation), methane, and other gases are causing a greenhouse effect. In what many fear is a harbinger of the warming, the eighties were the warmest decade on record. Seven of the eight warmest years on record have occurred since 1980, with 1990 and 1991 the two warmest yet. Without rapid action by the world community, there will likely be catastrophic effects within decades, including severe water shortages, lowered agricultural production in important food producing regions, destruction of coral reefs and northern forests, and a sea-level rise that could swamp coastal cities or even entire countries, such as the low-lying Maldives in the Indian Ocean.[18]

The climate issue poses many of the same challenges as did ozone depletion, but on a far more imposing scale. They include a significant dose of scientific complexity and uncertainty, considerable tensions between industrialized and developing countries over responsibility and blame, and a threat to entrenched industries. Negotiations toward an international climate treaty began in February, 1991 in Chantilly, Virginia, and were expected to lead to the signing of at least a "framework convention"—a statement of intention to cooperate on research and take concrete action in the future—by the Rio conference. As with both the European air pollution treaties and the ozone effort, however, agreeing to a framework treaty is likely to be merely the beginning of a long—perhaps dangerously long—process of forging international consensus.[19]

The second global commons is comprised of the oceans and seas, and of rivers that cross from one country to another. International treaties have reduced the dumping of toxic chemicals in the North Sea, curtailed ocean dumping and vessel discharges, and slowed fishstock depletions in some areas. There has been some progress in achieving recognition of the seas as a common heritage, but that progress has been painfully slow—and for determined transgressors, still leaves the seas largely vulnerable to exploitation.

The Law of the Sea treaty of 1982 was an attempt to lay down some guidelines for use of the oceans. It was the product of ten years of painstaking negotiations. The treaty granted coastal nations the right to control resource development within 200 miles (325 kilometers) of their shores. It also obligated them, in exchange for this right, to protect the marine environments in areas under their control. Those ratifying the convention are expected to participate in treaties aimed at controlling pollution from agricultural runoff, discharges from cities, ocean dumping, transport of hazardous materials, emergency response to accidents, releases from boats, oil exploration and drilling, mining, and air pollutants falling into the ocean. In all of these areas, nations have willingly accepted international constraints on domestic actions in order to reap the environmental rewards.[20]

Another major element of the Law of the Sea negotiations was an agreement to regard the deep seabed and its resources as the "common heritage of mankind." The convention called for the creation of an International Seabed Authority that would cooperatively mine the deep seabed for minerals if it became economically attractive to do so. As part of the bargain, industrial countries agreed to provide some of the needed mining technology. Private mining ventures would be licensed, with a share of the revenues going to developing countries in recognition of their stake in the global resource. Though the seabed provisions were hailed by many observers as an historic jump in international cooperation, they proved to be a major impediment to worldwide acceptance of the treaty. Several industrial countries have refused to sign or ratify the convention without changes in these controversial sections.[21]

As a result, a decade after its completion, the Law of the Sea still has not entered into force because only 51 of the 60 countries required under the treaty's own terms have ratified it. Ironically, the seabed mining provisions have proved to be something of a period piece. No deep seabed mining is likely to take place for several decades, at least, and few geologists still view the ocean floor as a pot of gold. Given these changed circumstances and a moderation in developing country attitudes, some supporters of the treaty hope that it can now be revised to eliminate the controversial provisions so that the United States and other holdouts will ratify. Though the treaty is not in force, many of its provisions are now observed as customary international law, with positive effects on fish stocks, ocean pollution, and navigational freedoms.[22]

Considerable progress has also been made in the joint management of seas shared by several countries. UNEP's "regional seas" program, developed in the early seventies, has led to agreements on 10 seas that are together shared by more than 120 nations. The agreements provide for data gathering, cooperative long-term planning, and the negotiation of legally binding treaties. In several cases, hostile nations have been able to work together toward this goal. The Mediterranean Action Plan, for example, has elicited collaboration between such traditional enemies as Israel and Lebanon.[23]

But while this cooperation has proven invaluable, few of the regions involved have yet developed binding accords on pressing priorities such as reducing sewage and agricultural runoff and other land-based sources of pollution. And in the regional seas program, as with so many other international efforts, a chronic problem has been a lack of sustained financing once the original seed money runs out.[24]

17

Outside the auspices of the regional seas program, three independent treaties—protecting the North Sea and the Baltic—took effect in the seventies. The North Sea, between Britain, northern Europe and Scandinavia, had suffered heavily from the dumping of everything from municipal sewage to industrial toxics. The Oslo convention of 1972 curtailed North Sea dumping, and the Paris convention of 1974 placed controls on land-based sources of pollution. Also in 1974, delegates met in Helsinki to give similar protections to the Baltic Sea. These treaties had measurable effects. For instance, the dumping of titanium dioxide in the North Sea fell by 42 percent between 1979 and 1989. In the Baltic, PCBs have been reduced moderately, and DDT levels have fallen sharply.[25]

International law has been prolific, but less beneficial to the environment, in the management of rivers that cross national borders. Though concerns about shared watercourses have generated more than 2,000 treaties, these agreements generally focus on navigation rights and give little attention to either the pollution or allocation of water.[26]

One exception is a UNEP-initiated program to develop an action plan for the cooperative management of the Zambezi River in southern Africa, which provides water for more than 20 million people in eight countries. The plan includes provisions for information exchange and other cooperative programs that will ultimately be backed up by a legally binding convention. UNEP hopes the Zambezi plan will serve as a model for future agreements covering other river basins.[27]

In another important initiative, members of the ECE are now using their air pollution experience to develop a treaty regulating pollution and allocation issues for regional rivers and other watercourses. Participating countries will be obligated to prevent and control pollution of waterways and to cooperate on monitoring, research and development, early warning systems, and information exchange. Protocols containing more concrete targets will then be negotiated for individual rivers and lakes. The treaty was expected to be open for signature in February, 1992.[28]

A third area of common resources—and one of the most threatened—is the biological diversity on which all ecosystems depend. Although nations harboring a large share of this heritage resist the notion that it is anything but their sovereign property, the erosion of biological diversity impoverishes the whole world and is thus a global concern. At the international level, several efforts have been made to preserve ecosystems and wildlife, yet the decimation of habitats and species has continued at a tragic rate.

Here, as with other moves toward environmental governance, progress has been stalled by a lack of funding. The 1971 Convention on Wetlands of International Importance (known as Ramsar, after the city in Iran where it was concluded), for example, obligates the 61 participating nations to list designated wetlands within their territory, to promote their conservation, and to establish nature reserves in important ones. But because it created no fund to help finance the preservation, few developing countries participate in it. The 1972 World Heritage Convention, signed by more than 100 countries, created a list of important cultural and biological sites meriting protection and theoretically provided a fund for managing them—but nations have not contributed enough money to it to make an appreciable dent in the problem.[29]

The 1973 Washington Convention on Trade in Endangered Species (CITES), on the other hand, is a relative success story. Signed by more than 100 countries, CITES restricts the import and export of endangered wild animals and plants and products made from them. It prohibits entirely any trade involving species threatened with extinction, as with a ban on the ivory trade it imposed in 1990 to protect the African elephant. Another notable wildlife agreement was a 1982 agreement by the International Whaling Commission to outlaw commercial whaling by 1986. However, the future of this ban was jeopardized in December, 1991, when Iceland announced it was withdrawing from the Commission in order to resume the catch.[30]

Though these treaties have accomplished some good, much stronger protections will be required if the exponential loss of the earth's biological diversity is to be not only slowed, but stopped. By the estimate of one leading biologist, 5 to 10 percent of the world's species may be lost per decade over the next quarter century. So far, the world community has focussed disproportionately on well-known wildlife and neglected the millions of small plants and animals that underpin ecosystems—and may harbor much-needed medical treatments or important agricultural strains. The negotiations now underway toward an umbrella biodiversity treaty thus aim to go beyond existing agreements in order to adequately preserve rapidly dwindling genetic resources.[31]

Key to any successful agreement will be adequate provisions for financing conservation. Part of the solution may be to grant the local communities who control genetic resources some form of intellectual property rights to them. Northern pharmaceutical and seed companies benefiting from third world genes would thus pay local people for extraction rights, thereby helping to finance preservation. In one promising private initiative along these lines, Merck & Co., the world's largest pharmaceutical company, has agreed to pay the National Institute of Biodiversity of Costa Rica $1 million to be channeled into conservation efforts in exchange for access to the country's plants, microbes, and insects. Should any product become marketable, Merck has agreed to pay the institute a share of the royalties. A key to success in this and other similar ventures will be insuring that benefits flow to the local level. Paradoxically, protecting a common resource in this case involves recognizing that not all countries have an equal claim to it. In exchange for protecting their resource for the common good, communities and nations who harbor biological diversity have the right to remuneration for profits made from it.[32]

Reaching agreements to preserve tropical forests, which harbor a significant share of the earth's biological riches in addition to playing a crucial role in regulating climate, is a pressing priority. The earth's forest cover is rapidly diminishing, with an estimated 17 million hectares lost per year—an area twice the size of Austria. A tropical forestry action plan developed by the United Nations Development Programme, the U.N. Food and Agricultural Organization, the World Bank, and World Resources Institute in the mid-eighties has so far failed to slow the losses, though it is now being revamped. At the 1990 economic summit, U.S.

President George Bush proposed that a global forest treaty be negotiated. However, the talks over this agreement have been put on hold, largely because of opposition by some developing countries and a reluctance on the part of the industrial countries to agree to provide the kind of financial help needed to pay for the preservation of forests in developing countries.[33]

Despite this reluctance, progress is being made on the establishment of a fund to preserve the tropical forests of one country—Brazil. In 1990, Germany's Chancellor Helmut Kohl recommended setting up a sizable fund that would create large reserves in the Amazon and help to identify new, environmentally sound work for the ranchers, farmers, loggers, and others who live in the rainforest. The funding governments see this as a pilot effort that could be extended to other countries. So far, industrialized countries have pledged more than $250 million for the first phase of the project, which will be under the joint management of the Brazilian government, the European Community, and the World Bank. This kind of support is an important acknowledgment that if major global resources are to be saved, the wealthier nations will have to help defray the costs. However, the fund's usefulness will depend greatly on whether the people who live in the forests are full participants in its design and implementation.[34]

A different kind of commons is comprised of territories under international stewardship. The continent of Antarctica is generally recognized as a common because governments have found it easier to do this than to decide which countries could lay legitimate claim to it. When the original Antarctica treaty was signed in 1959, seven different countries had actually put down their flags on Antarctica. They and five other nations agreed to put aside all claims and jointly manage the continent "in the interests of all mankind." More specifically, the signatories banned all military activities, nuclear tests, and radioactive wastes from the continent and agreed to promote international scientific cooperation there. In the years since, treaty members have issued hundreds of regulations on issues such as the designation of protected areas and disposal of wastes. They have also negotiated companion treaties on protecting seals and conserving other Antarctic marine resources.[35]

A recent agreement, reached in 1991, bans all mining exploration and

> "The global economy is subject to some of the same kinds of abuses—and poses the same needs for physical constraints—as the physical and biological systems with which it is inextricably bound."

development for fifty years, at which time it will be difficult but not impossible to "walk away" from the agreement. This new accord over-turns an earlier convention that would have regulated mining should it occur. The agreement also puts in place an array of environmental pro-tection measures, including environmental impact assessment require-ments, provisions on the handling of native plants and animals, waste management requirements, and the creation of an advisory Committee for Environmental Protection.[36]

However, one contentious aspect of the Antarctica treaty remains: the limited membership of the "Antarctica club." The treaty's founding sig-natories have restricted membership to those who carry out scientific research on the continent. There are now 40 members, of whom 26 are "consultative parties" with full decision-making rights and 14 are observers. Developing countries resent that the membership conditions exclude many of them, as they lack the resources to conduct scientific research in Antarctica. In the Third World view, the "common heritage of mankind" is being held in trust by a very limited segment of the world community.[37]

A fifth category of commons is the global economy. While not a physical feature of the earth itself, it is nonetheless subject to some of the same kinds of abuses—and poses the same needs for mutual constraints—as the physical and biological systems with which it is inextricably bound. For example, just as the oceans have been used as receptacles for waste, export practices have been used to "solve" problems for individual countries or industries in a way that only creates larger problems for the world as a whole.

In the wake of the revelations in Koko, Nigeria and several other inci-dents in 1988, UNEP accelerated talks aimed at regulating the export of hazardous industrial and municipal wastes. These talks led to the 1989 Basel Convention, which calls for nations to adhere to a system known as "prior informed consent," whereby a country planning such exports has to obtain the permission of the receiving country before the ship-ment can proceed. The U.N. Food and Agriculture Organization and UNEP devised a similar system of voluntary prior informed consent for the export of chemicals and pesticides that are banned or restricted in five or more countries. Participants are currently working out the details of the program, which is expected to be functioning soon.[38]

Although these "informed consent" systems may be better than nothing, many environmental groups and developing country governments would prefer total bans on the export of hazardous wastes and products, believing that to regulate this trade is to legitimize it. Some exporting countries argue that bans violate an importer's sovereign right to decide if it wishes to accept the risk in exchange for either cash or the supposed benefits of the restricted product. However, in the debate over the Basel Accord, many Third World countries argued strenuously in favor of a ban, which suggests that they are not particularly worried about losing this particular "right."[39]

As a result of widespread dissatisfaction with the informed consent approach, many countries have now moved toward stronger measures. The European Community (EC) agreed in March, 1990 to stop exporting waste to the 69 countries in Africa, the Caribbean, and the Pacific that are former colonies of EC members. In return, the former colonies agreed to ban waste imports. The Bamako Convention, signed in February, 1991 by 10 African countries, bans waste imports to the African continent.[40]

In the most extreme form of dangerous exports, whole industries sometimes move to parts of the world where environmental regulations are relatively lenient. Products can be shipped back to the head office's home country, meaning that consumers get the benefit of the product while shifting the environmental costs onto others. In some cases, manufacturers who stay put and comply with domestic environmental laws can find themselves at a competitive disadvantage. The world community has not yet devised a solution to this dilemma, though world trade bodies are beginning to wrestle with the issue.[41]

Forging Stronger Treaties

Though nations have achieved some notable successes in international environmental governance, the problems are growing worse at a rate that threatens to overwhelm incremental progress. Unfortunately, international diplomacy is a slow business. Most treaties take years and years to negotiate, ratify, and implement. The disparate interests and conditions of individual nations tend to create a least-common-denominator effect, in which treaties reflect the desires of the most reluctant state. And even the relatively weak treaties now in force rarely include effective means of ensuring that the governments signing them will meet their obligations. However, the past twenty years' experience has yielded some instructive lessons in environmental negotiations—which the world community can now apply to the far larger challenges looming on the horizon.

23

Paradoxically, one way to make environmental agreements more effective is in some cases to make them less enforceable—and therefore more palatable to negotiators who may initially feel threatened by any loss of sovereignty. So-called "soft law"—declarations, resolutions, and action plans that nations do not need to formally ratify and are not legally binding—can help to create an international consensus, mobilize aid, and lay the groundwork for the negotiation of binding treaties later. This approach has been used successfully in many areas, such as UNEP's regional seas program. "Agenda 21", an action plan on nearly all aspects of sustainable development expected to emerge from UNCED, would fall into this category.[42]

When a binding treaty is necessary, the "convention-protocol" approach, which was used in both the transboundary air pollution and the ozone talks, is now the dominant model. Under this approach, a "framework" treaty is agreed to first, that generally does not involve any binding commitment, but represents a political commitment to take action at a later date. It also strengthens the joint research and monitoring programs needed to build enough scientific consensus and knowledge to convince countries to eventually commit to specific targets. The framework treaty is then followed by specific protocols on various aspects of the problem. The subject of a given protocol is often deliberately limited in order to facilitate agreement.

In the transboundary air pollution case, the monitoring set in motion by the 1979 convention revealed an extensive trade in emissions. It found, for instance, that Austria and Norway both import more than ninety percent of the sulfur deposited within their territory, and that even West Germany, long thought to be a culprit more than a victim in the transboundary trade, was importing more than two-thirds of the sulfur threatening its forests. This new data spurred progress by confirming that most countries, not just the few obvious victims, had an interest in an agreement. In the ozone talks as well, a 1985 framework convention created a forum for international scientific cooperation, which helped create the consensus needed for countries to commit to reductions.[43]

Though these are real advantages, there is also a danger that letting countries sign a framework treaty without requiring any firm promises provides an easy political out that can delay progress toward actual reductions. Jim MacNeill, the former Secretary General of the World Commission on Environment and Development, notes: "An empty framework convention enables our leaders to cop out of these discussions and gain credit for doing so.... It is much like an author going to a publisher with a table of contents, asking for an advance and getting it on the promise that his children or grandchildren will write the narrative." One protection against this kind of "cop-out" is to require that any country signing a framework treaty be bound to accept at least one specific protocol at the same time, as required in UNEP's regional seas program.[44]

Another way to spur progress is for countries or groups of countries to make voluntary pledges or take unilateral actions. During the European acid rain debate, a "30-percent club" of European countries committed informally to a 30-percent reduction in sulfur dioxide emissions. This helped create the political will for a binding treaty. In the ozone discussions, early U.S. leadership was an important factor. According to the U.S. chief negotiator for the ozone talks, Richard Eliot Benedick, the United States persistently urged the reluctant Europeans, Japanese, and Soviets to act. He gave much of the credit to an informed and vocal public, which had already succeeded in forcing the passage of the strictest national ozone protection legislation in the world. American industry, in turn, came to favor international regulation over national laws in order to level the global playing field. Similarly, in the global warming talks, Germany created momentum by vowing to cut its carbon emissions 25 percent by 2005. This spurred the European Community to commit to stabilizing carbon emissions by the year 2000. It remains to be seen if this will create enough pressure to convince the United States to follow suit.[45]

A sustained commitment by international organizations can be critical to success. Observers to both the ozone talks and the negotiations over

the Basel Accord cite the personal intervention of UNEP head
Mostafa Tolba as important to reaching consensus. By working behind
the scenes, Tolba was able to bridge differences between nations.
International non-governmental organizations (NGOs) also help to spur
progress. In the ozone negotiations, according to Benedick, NGOs were
able to form a consensus for action that transcended parochial national
interests. Organizations such as Friends of the Earth, Greenpeace
International, and the Natural Resources Defense Council were particularly active. Groups like the International Climate Action Network, the
World Rainforest Network, and others that bring together environmentalists from around the globe to lobby during negotiations, will be essential to building pressure for stronger treaties. While NGOs are not
routinely granted the right to intervene in international deliberations,
they have been allowed to do so to a limited degree in the preparations
for UNCED and in the climate talks.[46]

Domestic political developments can also be crucial to the prospects for
a treaty. An impressive showing by Green parties in Australia and
France in 1989 led to a dramatic about-face in the negotiations over mining in Antarctica, when Australia and then France announced that they
would not sign the Wellington Convention that would have allowed
mining. This doomed the convention, as the accession of both countries
was required because they were among the seven countries with original
territorial claims there. Other key countries, including Japan, the United
Kingdom, and—at the last minute—the United States—began shifting
their positions as it became clear that the Wellington convention was
dead. In the early months of 1992, environmentalists in the United States
were hoping that the prospect of the November presidential election
would make it difficult for President Bush to remain oblivious to the
Earth Summit and the treaties expected to be signed there.[47]

Sometimes a new piece of scientific information or some dramatic experience drives the process forward. For instance, the discovery of a hole
in the ozone layer over Antarctica in May, 1985 added political impetus
for countries to agree to the Montreal Protocol, and the scorching summer of 1988, when drought-like conditions in many parts of the world
led to tightened world food supplies, alerted the world to the global
warming threat and set in motion an international fact-gathering process
that quickly led to international negotiations. Similarly, a spate of dra-

matic instances of hazardous waste exports during 1988 drove the negotiations on the Basel Accord forward at record speed. The Exxon Valdez oil spill in Alaska, along with Australia's and France's about-face, helped to tip the political balance in favor of a mining ban in Antarctica by dramatically demonstrating the potential for catastrophic accidents in sensitive environments.[48]

Occasionally, efforts to negotiate environmental treaties are hindered by a "blocking coalition"— a group of nations that tries to prevent the creation of a strong treaty. If these countries are essential to addressing the issue at hand, their opposition can be fatal. Sometimes, only one country—a "veto state"—can scuttle an agreement. Reversals of position by this government can then become critical. In the acid rain negotiations, for example, Germany blocked agreement as a veto state, until the discovery that its forests were dying convinced its delegates to change their minds. In the global warming talks, the United States still wears the veto-state mantle. The priority then is to influence the veto state or the members of the blocking coalition, through both international political persuasion and domestic public pressure.[49]

Countries favoring a treaty can sometimes tip the balance by offering incentives to a reluctant participant. The Montreal Protocol, for example, granted deferrals in CFC reduction commitments to developing countries, to make the phase-down less economically onerous. Perhaps the single most important factor in the treaty's success, however, was the creation of a fund to help the poorer countries make the transition to CFC substitutes—a lesson that can well be applied to treaties on biodiversity and climate, and to the Earth Summit. Key developing countries such as China would not have supported the Montreal treaty had its call for technical and financial assistance not been heeded. Growing CFC use in non-signatory nations could then have overwhelmed reductions by treaty signers. Unfortunately, the fund is off to a slow start, with only $35 million of the $53 million pledged for 1991 having been raised as of February, 1992.[50]

In addition to using such inducements as the ozone fund, supporters of a pending treaty may sometimes need to use the spur of trade sanctions. For instance, the U.S. threatened an embargo against Japan if it refused to participate in the 1982 commercial whaling ban. It also threatened to

> "Perhaps the single most important factor in the ozone treaty's success was the creation of a fund to help the poorer countries make the transition to CFC substitutes."

embargo any fish caught by driftnet, in order to secure Japanese and Taiwanese agreement to a December, 1991 United Nations resolution reaffirming an international commitment to stop using driftnets for fishing by the end of 1992. The Montreal Protocol uses a similar tool, though internationally rather than unilaterally imposed. Parties to the protocol are simply forbidden to purchase CFCs (or products made from them) from non-signatories. This rule negates any incentive not to sign the protocol in order to make windfall profits, and thereby helps to prevent shifts of production from one country to another in order to escape regulation.[51]

27

Once a treaty is agreed to, there is a need for effective provisions for updating it should new scientific information or shifting political winds make a stronger agreement possible. The ozone story demonstrates the value of having such a provision. The ink was barely dry on the treaty when worrisome new evidence emerged. Ozone depletion was already taking place over the heavily populated northern hemisphere. Furthermore, the new data suggested that the atmospheric models assumed in preparing the Montreal Protocol had underestimated the pace of depletion—and that dangerous amounts of ozone loss would occur even if all nations fully implemented the treaty. The Montreal agreement contained a provision allowing it to be updated in some cases through revisions to its annex, without having to ratify a whole new treaty. Such revisions are automatically binding unless one party to the treaty expressly objects. Thus the 1990 decision to phase CFCs out entirely was able to take effect immediately, with no need for another extended ratification process. The new information on still more accelerated rates of depletion is likely to hasten yet another revision.[52]

Another way to build in flexibility for future updating of a treaty is to delegate the power to set environmental standards to the governing bodies for a treaty. The standards can then be adapted to changing conditions. These bodies, composed of representatives of member states, can sometimes agree to set standards by two-thirds majority (or some other formula) rather than by unanimous vote. This helps overcome the least-common-denominator problem. The governing bodies of the marine pollution accords, among other agreements, have this power. The majority voting procedures in the International Whaling Commission, for example, made it possible to pass a ban in spite of the vociferous opposition of key whaling states like Japan, Iceland, and Norway. Some international institutions, such as the International Labour Organisation (ILO), provide a forum through which governments can set standards on an ongoing basis. Other agencies set voluntary standards themselves, such as air pollution standards established by the World Health Organization. Though these are non-binding guidelines, countries look to them as the internationally-recognized norm.[53]

Improving Compliance

Reaching agreement on a treaty is only half the battle; the other half is seeing that countries stand by their signatures. Unlike national governments, international agencies do not have police powers. Most treaties do not even stipulate any sanctions. And partly because there is little enforcement, there is little data on compliance. But Abram and Antonia Chayes, professors of international law at Harvard and Georgetown Universities, find that "there is no reason to think that fulfillment by states of their international obligations compares unfavorably to compliance with domestic legal rules—certainly not with those covering the distribution or use of narcotic drugs or even the payment of taxes." Though this suggests that most countries take their treaty commitments at least somewhat seriously, the comparison to widely flouted domestic legislation also suggests that there is vast room for improvement. Discouraging confirmation comes from data the Norwegian environmental group Bellona recently compiled showing that Norway— widely viewed as a world leader on international environmental issues—is likely to fall short of meeting its commitments in 12 of the 27 major international agreements to which it is a party.[54]

A powerful way to encourage compliance is to require collection of pertinent data, and to make this data available to all interested parties. Nations are sometimes required to submit detailed annual reports both on data directly relevant to the treaty, and on actions they have taken to comply. In the acid rain accords, for example, the participating nations must report their sulfur dioxide emissions. Treaty secretariats, if they have the resources, can keep tabs on compliance and bring breaches to the attention of other governments. If the information is made public,

> **"Most countries will not want to take on international commitments that might undermine their economic position unless they are certain that everyone is playing by the same rules."**

NGOs and others can shine a spotlight on those countries that have not followed through on commitments. For instance, University of Massachusetts political scientist Peter Haas finds that the data gathering efforts mandated by the Baltic and North Sea treaties have enabled environmental groups such as Greenpeace to call public attention to nations that are particular offenders.[55]

Unfortunately, making freedom of environmental information a reality is often a difficult struggle. During the ozone talks, Greenpeace waged a long and only partially successful battle to make CFC production and trade data publicly available. Under the Antarctic treaties, documents were restricted for decades, and meetings were closed. Only under outside pressure has the cloak of secrecy recently begun to lift.[56]

In some cases, monitoring and inspections may be necessary to ensure that governments are keeping their word. This is particularly the case for agreements that cover economically important activities; most countries will not want to take on international commitments that might undermine their economic position unless they are certain that everyone is playing by the same rules. A few environmental agreements already provide for inspections to insure compliance. For example, under the 1973 International Convention for the Prevention of Pollution from Ships (MARPOL), countries may inspect ships visiting their ports from other countries to see that the provisions of the treaty are being respected. The Law of the Sea Treaty has more extensive provisions for inspections that allow countries to enforce international standards within their 200-mile limit. Under the 1959 Antarctica Treaty, member countries are allowed to conduct unannounced inspections of bases set up by other countries, to insure that the treaty rules are being obeyed.[57]

The International Atomic Energy Agency also conducts inspections, under the Nuclear Non-Proliferation Treaty, to ensure that radioactive waste from civilian nuclear power plants—which can be used to make nuclear bombs—is not being diverted toward military ends. But the 1991 discovery that Iraq, a treaty signatory, was well on its way to developing a bomb despite the inspections demonstrates the need to strengthen the system—possibly by providing for unannounced visits. Provisions for on-site inspections in arms control agreements such as the INF and START treaties have also broken new ground in this area, establishing precedents that may one day prove helpful to international environmental agreements.[58]

Nations may in the future rely increasingly on satellites to monitor environmental actions, as is already happening in a U.S. government effort to enforce compliance with bilateral agreements covering the use of driftnets in the Northern Pacific Ocean between the United States and Japan, South Korea, and Taiwan. Fishing boats equipped with driftnets are required to carry radio transmitters so that their movements can be tracked. When the monitors detect patterns that suggest the presence of a boat fishing in areas forbidden under the agreements, coast guard officials are allowed to board the suspicious vessel and detain it if necessary until the appropriate national authority arrives on the scene. According to Alan Major of the U.S. National Marine Fisheries Service, the system has been effective in preventing pirate vessels from fishing illegally. But its future is now in some doubt, as the bilateral agreements are to expire when the U.N.-dictated moratorium on driftnet fishing takes effect at the end of 1992.[59]

Occasionally, sanctions will be needed not only to encourage participation in an agreement but to punish participants who violate it blatantly; the deliberate setting of the oil fires in Kuwait shows that the earth's environment is still highly vulnerable to abuse by rogue nations. The most practical options are trade sanctions, which are prescribed by a growing number of treaties. For example, countries party to CITES recently imposed an international ban on the purchase of wildlife products from Thailand on the grounds that illegal traders were shipping goods such as ivory from Africa, caiman skins from Latin America, and orangutans and palm cockatoos from Indonesia through that country. An early 1991 report from the U.S. International Trade Commission identifies 19 international environmental agreements that use some form of trade sanction to improve compliance. In another type of sanction, a 1989 treaty outlawing the use of driftnets in the South Pacific requires countries to revoke the "good standing" listing on a regional register of vessels engaged in driftnet fishing. Countries can then deny the blacklisted vessel acccess to their fishing grounds.[60]

Effectively implementing stronger treaties will necessitate the use of carrots, as well as sticks. In the poorer nations, critical shortages—both of

> "The deliberate setting of the oil fires in Kuwait shows that the earth's environment is still highly vulnerable to abuse by rogue nations."

investment capital and of access to environmentally beneficial technologies—can make compliance impossible even with the best of intentions. In such cases, one of the most practical means of enabling developing countries to participate fully in a treaty is to create an international fund to cover the costs. The creation of the ozone fund set a useful precedent. One important provision of its rules stipulates that assistance from the fund depends on good-faith efforts to comply with the treaty's terms. Though there is wide recognition that similar arrangements will be needed for future treaties on biodiversity, global warming, and the Earth Summit's Agenda 21, industrial-country reluctance to commit to adequate sums is proving to be a major barrier.[61]

Beyond establishing a source of funding, governments need to facilitate the transfer of needed technologies by other means. One common problem is that private ownership of patents in industrial countries makes it difficult for governments to transfer technology on noncommercial terms. Given this conundrum, industrial countries are emphasizing that many useful technologies are publicly held. What remains largely missing is the institutional framework needed to facilitate cooperation and exchange information between those who control technologies and those who need them.[62]

Strengthening Environmental Institutions

To improve the current highly laborious and piece-meal process of international environmental governance, stronger institutions are needed to help negotiate treaties, implement them, settle disputes over their terms, and dispense the financial and technological assistance required to make them work.

The time may be ripe not only to adopt majority voting provisions within the individual governing bodies for treaties, but to establish a central negotiating forum. Under existing practice, a new international committee—such as the International Negotiating Committee on Climate Change—is created nearly every time a major treaty is up for discussion. A unified forum could greatly improve the efficiency and dispatch with which rapidly-escalating global problems are addressed. A possible model for a standing environmental negotiating body would be an institution such as the General Agreement on Tariffs and Trade (GATT) or the International Monetary Fund (IMF), which serve similar functions in the economic arena.[63]

Once treaties are agreed to, nations will need to delegate to international institutions the task of seeing that they are implemented. As a first step, signatory nations could give treaty secretariats (small offices set up by governments to administer treaties) the mandate and resources to monitor compliance. A recent U.S. General Accounting Office review of eight major international environmental agreements found that the participating countries do not always present the treaty secretariats with complete and timely information as required. The secretariats generally do not have the wherewithal or authority to verify reported information, or to independently monitor for compliance. A typical secretariat employs fewer than twenty individuals and has an annual budget of $1-3 million, a drop in the bucket compared, for example, to the budgets of such domestic programs as the $408 million allocated to the U.S. Environmental Protection Agency for its air quality operations.[64]

A notable exception is the CITES (endangered species) secretariat, which despite limited resources, has considerable powers—and uses them with widely-acknowledged effectiveness. It has, for example, the power to request information from countries about alleged lapses, and to demand explanations from countries it believes are falling short of meeting treaty obligations. The record of CITES shows how effective a treaty secretariat can be when participating countries are willing to delegate the needed powers, and to back those powers by imposing trade sanctions if necessary.[65]

International institutions that have successfully administered agreements in other (non-environmental) fields can serve as useful models for the environmental sphere. Both the United Nations and European Commissions on Human Rights have powers to monitor compliance and to demand explanations from signatories for reported lapses. The ILO also keeps tabs on whether members are following through on their obligations. Under a two-stage process, the ILO can often generate enough pressure in the first, investigatory, stage to bring an errant country into line, making the second stage—a public hearing to explain lapses—unnecessary. Both management and labor actually form part of the governing body of the ILO through a unique tripartite system in which these groups share equal standing with governments. The human rights commissions and the ILO both rely on NGOs for help in identifying violators.[66]

When disputes arise, an internationally accepted means of determining whether or not a country is abiding by its environmental treaty commitments is needed—an international judiciary. The Law of the Sea provides one possible model for a dispute settlement system. In some cases, under that treaty, national courts could simply be opened to foreign claims. In others, international procedures would apply, ranging from informal consultation to compulsory binding judicial proceedings. In the latter case, countries are offered four options, including the World Court, a special Law of the Sea tribunal, and two types of arbitration. In a special seabed chamber of the tribunal, corporations and individuals would have legal standing. In a more recent initiative, Austria, Czechoslovakia, Hungary, Italy, Poland, and Yugoslavia have proposed to UNCED that an inquiry commission be created under which countries would participate in fact-finding and information gathering processes and choose from a variety of negotiation and conciliation techniques to try to settle their differences. The proposal appears to be picking up support.[67]

The International Court of Justice (the World Court) at the Hague could be an important dispute settlement tool if used as originally intended. At present, most treaties provide for voluntary rather than mandatory use of the World Court to resolve disputes involving international obligations, and most nations have not agreed to have disputes against them heard at the World Court without their consent. Granting the Court more automatic jurisdiction, and giving international organizations and NGOs the right to initiate suits, would markedly improve its usefulness. Under these circumstances, enough cases might even be brought to merit the creation of a special environmental chamber. The European Community has already demonstrated the utility of an international judiciary. Countries accused of violating EC laws— environmental and otherwise—are brought before the European Court. Though it does not yet have the power to impose sanctions, the public shaming resulting from a negative ruling is often sufficient to prompt change.[68]

In many cases, as has been noted, bringing countries into compliance will involve providing financial and technological assistance rather than imposing punitive measures. This function, like the treaty-making and judicial ones, will require institutional coordination. One candidate for this role is the $1.3-billion Global Environment Facility (GEF) based in Washington, D.C. It was set up in late 1990 to finance environmental projects in developing countries, that would help address global ecological ills. The fund is under the joint management of the World Bank, UNEP, and UNDP. It concentrates on projects to slow global warming, preserve biodiversity, protect international waters, and combat ozone depletion. Industrial countries look to it as the logical institution to manage future trust funds created under any new treaties, an arrangement now being considered for the ozone fund.[69]

One difficulty with the GEF, however, is that developing countries would prefer any "green funds" to be independent of the World Bank, which they perceive to be in the pocket of the industrial world. Even some donor countries are beginning to acknowledge the need to develop more democratic decision making procedures for future green funds in order to give recipient countries more control. There is precedent for this in the voting procedures now in place for the ozone fund, in which industrialized and developing countries have equal weight. One idea being floated is linking a country's voting weight to the size of its ecological assets as well as to traditional economic criteria. This would be a recognition that countries like Brazil— rich in biological diversity and tropical forests—deserve considerable say in a fund's management. Beside changing its governance mechanism, the GEF—if it is to succeed—will also need to distance itself from the World Bank's reputation for secrecy and its penchant for large development projects that do not involve local people in their design or implementation.[70]

Another needed institutional role is reviewing whether or not treaties are fulfilling their intended functions—which sometimes may not be the case even if countries are obeying the letter of the law. For example, the 1972 World Heritage Convention was supposed to be a major step toward preserving areas of cultural or biological importance, but participating countries never contributed enough to the fund established by the convention to make its activities meaningful. If conventions were regularly reviewed for effectiveness, the international community could take steps to redress glaring deficiencies such as this. Some countries have proposed that a new governmental forum be created for this purpose at UNCED, perhaps assisted by non-governmental authorities in the field. Another possibility would be to leave the task wholly to non-governmental experts designated by governments.[71]

35

Governments and private groups have put forth a number of proposals to fill the gaps in the international institutional machinery, many of them in preparation for the Earth Summit. One motivation for some of the more far-reaching proposals is to fill the gap between the power granted the U.N.'s Security Council to take binding decisions and the meager authority given other U.N. organs. This power gap was established because the founders of the U.N. in 1945 deemed all matters except military security to be within the domestic jurisdiction of states. Now that it is clear that environmental matters cannot be contained within these boundaries, the U.N.'s institutional machinery must be brought into line with this new reality.[72]

Perhaps the most ambitious proposal yet came in the spring of 1989, when 17 heads of state signed a revolutionary though little-noticed document entitled the Declaration of the Hague. The leaders of countries as varied as Brazil, France, India, Japan, West Germany, and Zimbabwe all agreed that the problems of ozone depletion and global warming now require the creation of a new or newly strengthened institution within the U.N. system. This organization would be empowered to take decisions "even if, on occasion, unanimous agreement has not been achieved." The signers recognized that a requirement of unanimity is tantamount to a prescription for impasse. The new institution would also have the power to impose penalties for violations of international agreements. Disputes would be referred to the World Court for a binding settlement. Prime Minister Gro Harlem Brundtland of Norway concluded: "The principles we endorsed were radical, but any approach which is less ambitious would not serve us."[73]

The Hague Declaration is revolutionary because it goes well beyond traditional concepts of international law, which are based on the notion of a compact between sovereign states that cannot be bound to an international agreement without their express consent. But in a world with porous borders, countries are increasingly unable to control events within their own territory. And the treaty system now in place is unable to solve the problems, given its slow pace and the ability of a country that causes a large share of the problem either to not participate or to drag others down to the lowest common denominator. The Hague signatories were asserting that when it comes to the global environment, sovereignty must be "pooled" if it is to be exercised.[74]

Three years later, the Hague Declaration has slipped from sight. Its primary promoters, the heads of state of France, the Netherlands, and Norway, may simply have given up on the idea in the face of inevitable resistance from the United States and the former Soviet Union, which were not invited to the conference out of fear they would scuttle the deal. Overcoming the old rule of unanimous consent of states would, after all, require the very unanimity the Declaration itself was designed to overcome—an international relations Catch-22. Still, more than 30 nations eventually signed the Declaration. It thus represents the achievement of a remarkable degree of consensus on what must ultimately be done to save the planet.[75]

Since the Hague Declaration, nations and private analysts have made a number of other proposals for a high level forum through which governments can weigh and make decisions on environmental matters. For example, the United Kingdom suggested in 1989 that the existing Security Council could be used to discuss environmental matters with security implications, such as the Chernobyl nuclear disaster. But countries that are not members of the Security Council resist the idea that it should be central to environmental decisionmaking. Another proposal, advocated at times by Norway, the former Soviet Union, and the United Kingdom, would be to create an environmental security council to respond to environmental emergencies and their consequences. Other ideas include creating a new committee of the General Assembly to handle issues of sustainable development, reforming the Economic and Social Council (ECOSOC) so that it could do the job, and giving the task to the Trusteeship Council, originally created to assist countries with decolonization, and now in need of a new mission.[76]

Another key objective of many of the proposals is to merge the U.N.'s environment and development capacities so that the system takes account of the linkages between them, and promotes sustainable development. Toward this end, the United States has proposed to UNCED that a moribund environmental coordination board be revived, composed of high-level representatives of relevant specialized agencies, particularly UNEP and UNDP. The United Nations Association of the United States suggests that a small, high-level board be created from within ECOSOC to coordinate its work on sustainable development issues, and to provide some measure of authority over the work of the U.N.'s diverse specialized agencies in this area.[77]

Although it is difficult at the time of this writing (February, 1992) to know what will happen at the Earth Summit in Brazil, most observers expect that any reforms agreed to there will be primarily limited to existing institutions. UNEP is a prime candidate for strengthening. Created to catalyze environmental work throughout the U.N. system, it is widely acknowledged to have done a good job with the minimal resources the international community has put at its disposal. But its limited budget—until recently smaller than that of some U.S. environmental groups—is pitiful given the size of the task. An additional problem is UNEP's marginal position within the United Nations. Though it is charged with coordinating the U.N.'s response to environmental issues, it has little ability to influence the programs of other agencies with much larger budgets. It has no regulatory powers, and administers few programs.[78]

Governments are giving conspicuous lip-service to strengthening UNEP, but few of them seem to have a clear idea what this would mean. Some favor narrowing UNEP's priorities and focusing its efforts on those things they perceive it does best, such as data gathering and facilitating treaty negotiation. Others favor upgrading it to a specialized agency. At the very least, UNEP's budget is increasing. The organization's governing council (composed of contributing countries) recently approved a $150-million budget for 1992, up from $59 million in 1989—with further increases likely in the future.[79]

There remains some possibility that a new or recast institution with considerable powers will emerge from the Brazil conference. For instance, governments are considering various proposals to create a sustainable development commission to review environmental and development activities of the international system, and to monitor compliance with environmental treaties. Such a body, which might be modeled on the U.N. Commission on Human Rights, could be open to both official and non-governmental participation. There is also considerable discussion about the appropriate body to monitor follow-up to UNCED to see that effective programs—not just rhetoric—will emerge from commitments made there.[80]

Events in Rio also may lay the groundwork for a more ambitious reform of the United Nations proposed for 1995. An independent group of current and past world leaders including Willy Brandt, Jimmy Carter, Václav Havel, Julius Nyerere, and Eduard Shevardnadze has recommended that a World Summit on Global Governance be held that year—the fiftieth anniversary of the founding of the United Nations. In their statement, the Stockholm Initiative, they called for the summit to reexamine the organization's structure and operating procedures in light of altered world priorities and conditions since 1945. Decisions taken in 1995 would undoubtedly affect the way the United Nations handles environmental matters.[81]

For instance, one likely step is a review of the composition of the Security Council, whose permanent membership composed of the five post-World War II powers is hardly representative of today's world community. Only when the Council has broader representation can it seriously be considered as a forum where most international environmental conflicts might be addressed. Possibilities often mentioned as logical candidates for permanent Security Council seats include Brazil, the European Community, India, Japan, and Nigeria. The 1995 summit would also likely reconsider the requirement that decisions be made by unanimous vote in the Security Council, giving each permanent member a veto. Changing this rule would represent a fundamental transformation of international law on a par with that envisioned by the Hague Declaration.[82]

Most of the more ambitious reform proposals face a large hurdle—the need to revise the U.N. Charter if they are to be implemented. The present members of the Security Council are likely to strongly resist considering proposals that would require this, for fear of opening a "Pandora's box" that would result in the loss of much of their power.[83]

Reforming Economic Institutions

In national governments, the finance and commerce ministries often hold sway over environmental protection ministries in interagency

"Events in Rio may lay the groundwork for a more
ambitious reform of the United Nations
proposed for 1995."

struggles. At the international level as well, power rests with the institutions charged with managing the world economy. Strengthening global environmental governance will thus depend in large measure on substantially reforming today's leading international economic institutions—the World Bank, the International Monetary Fund, and the General Agreement on Tariffs and Trade.

39

These organizations have achieved considerable successes in the task granted them by governments when they were created after World War II—stabilizing the world monetary system and preventing a return to the protectionism of the thirties that contributed to the global depression. But the environment was not recognized to be inextricably linked with the economy at that time, as it is beginning to be now. The globalization of the world economy, combined with the power of the World Bank, IMF, and GATT to affect policies, means that a growing amount of *de facto* environmental governance is now taking place through the "back door"—via these organizations.

The World Bank exerts considerable influence in the countries to which it makes loans, through the projects it chooses to finance and the conditions it places on how the money is spent. All too often this influence has been negative, with the bank underwriting ecological debacles, such as large hydroelectric dams that have forced over a million people to relocate, and regional development programs that have stripped tropical rainforest. In recent years, its record has improved somewhat. In 1987, under pressure from environmental groups and the U.S. government, bank president Barber Conable announced several measures aimed at making sustainable development a greater priority throughout the bank's massive annual lending program ($23 billion in 1991). He created a central environment department and environmental units in each regional bureau, and announced that environmental impact assessments would be required for all projects. The amount of money devoted to free-standing environmental loans also began to increase. In 1991, such loans amounted to $1.6 billion, up from some $400 million in all previous years combined.[84]

Despite this progress, the bank has a long way to go before it can claim to have taken the sustainable development message to heart. The new environment department is committed to change, but it has so far had limited success in making its influence felt throughout the immense organization of nearly 6,000 employees in 53 offices around the world. By and large, the bank's ranks continue to be filled with economists who view environmental protection as an amenity rather than a fundamental precondition for sustainable development. Though the World Bank claims to be working to better integrate environmental concerns throughout its lending program, critics say that in many cases the environmental component of projects is so small as to border on irrelevance. And the bank continues to invest primarily in large, capital intensive projects that are relatively cheap to administer, rather than in the smaller-scale, grassroots efforts that are often needed. It also slows its own movement toward more enlightened lending practices by shrouding its operations in secrecy. The World Bank views itself as accountable to governments alone. As a result, local people and non-governmental groups cannot gain access to most of its documents, let alone participate in a meaningful way in the planning or implementation process—even though these documents may determine the fates of their communities.[85]

While the ecological impacts of the World Bank and regional development banks have received considerable attention in recent years, the IMF's environmental role has been largely overlooked. The fund was originally created to provide short-term balance of payments support for needy countries in order to help stabilize the world economic system. During the eighties, it played a central role in efforts to resolve the international debt crisis. In fiscal year 1991, the fund loaned out $20 billion. In return for access to IMF financing, the fund requires recipient countries to adopt "structural adjustment programs" that include a range of policy measures intended to set the recipient's economic house in order so that it will be creditworthy. Common policy prescriptions include steep cuts in government expenditures, reductions in subsidies, devaluation of currencies, and reduction of trade barriers.[86]

The products of often difficult negotiations between IMF officials and recipient governments, these programs have been roundly criticized in recent years. Many development experts and Third World governments charge that the reduced subsidies and slashed governmental expenditures generally prescribed in structural adjustment programs are a bitter medicine which usually hurts the poor disproportionately. In some cases, it is even questionable whether the programs are helpful to the country's economic health in the long run.[87]

"To the extent that structural adjustment programs hurt the poor, they will often also hurt the environment."

But the environment, too, can be a victim of IMF structural adjustment programs. The emphasis on boosting exports to earn foreign exchange can lead to the destruction of natural resources such as forests, wetlands, and mangroves, and to excessive development of ecologically damaging industries such as mining. Requirements that countries drastically reduce governmental expenditures can cause the elimination or postponement of crucial governmental activities, such as wildlife management or enforcement of environmental laws. Finally, to the extent that structural adjustment programs hurt the poor, they will often also hurt the environment, given the tendency for poverty and environmental degradation to go hand in hand. For instance, unemployed laborers might increasingly make their way into the tropical rainforest to engage in slash-and-burn agriculture.[88]

If environmental reform were treated as an important element of structural adjustment, these programs could be a powerful tool to encourage environmentally beneficial programs—while still achieving their original objectives of economic stabilization. Already, some policies promoted by structural adjustment programs are having positive environmental results. For instance, cutting subsidies to ecologically damaging industries, such as mining and energy development, helps to achieve both economic and environmental goals. A recent loan agreement with Haiti pointed out that government-imposed trade barriers on agricultural products were having the unintended effect of aggravating soil erosion by encouraging grain production on marginal lands. Removing the barriers, as the loan agreement recommended, would be an environmental gain. But at the moment, any environmental benefits are merely incidental by-products of the IMF's policy prescriptions rather than integral goals. Only when the fund's managers recognize that environmental health and economic prosperity are inextricably linked will this change.[89]

Unfortunately, the IMF is resisting even the most elementary environmental reforms. The U.S. Congress passed a bill in 1989 directing the U.S. treasury department to use its influence at the fund to promote such reforms, including the creation of an environmental department, procedures for more consultation with the public, and the weighing of environmental considerations in policy framework papers prepared jointly by the recipient country, the fund, and the World Bank. So far, however, the IMF has done little more than assign three economists to do environmental research. In February 1991, the fund's Executive Directors explicitly rejected the idea of creating an environment department. Environmental groups are lobbying Congress to turn down a proposed capital increase for the fund unless it begins to make environmental protection more of a priority.[90]

The international community is also beginning to pay attention, finally, to the effect of world trade agreements and institutions on the environment. Commercial interests, environmentalists, and government authorities alike have worried that new environmental policies might be on a collision course with free trade obligations. The question of how best to reconcile these goals has been debated for several years within the European Community, and emerged as a major issue in negotiations over a North American Free Trade Agreement in 1991. In addition, environmentalists have grown concerned that the current round of trade negotiations within GATT could lead to the erosion of hard-won environmental gains.

Their concern reached a crisis point with a September, 1991 ruling by a GATT dispute resolution panel suggesting that the use of trade sanctions for environmental purposes is at odds with GATT rules. The panel upheld a Mexican charge that a U.S. embargo on Mexican tuna violated GATT rules. The embargo had been imposed in accordance with a U.S. law that forbids the import of tuna from countries employing fishing practices that have been restricted at home because they fatally ensnare large numbers of dolphins along with the tuna. Consideration of the ruling by the full GATT General Council has been indefinitely deferred by joint agreement of the United States and Mexico. Yet the ruling itself was a clear signal that, unless GATT is amended, countries may encounter legal difficulties in using trade sanctions to promote environmental goals.[91]

There are many other ways in which free trade and environmental goals can conflict. Product standards can have the effect of discriminating against foreign-made products—such as cars not meeting domestic automobile fuel efficiency standards, or beverages sold in non-returnable bottles—whether or not this was their intent. Other important conservation strategies also can constrain trade. For example, some countries have banned the export of unprocessed logs, which hastens deforestation while creating few jobs. Japan, the leading importer of tropical logs from Southeast Asia, has charged that these bans violate GATT rules.[92]

Import taxes on products made in countries with lax environmental standards have also been attacked as trade barriers. The usual motivation for these taxes is to ensure that domestic producers are not put at a competitive disadvantage by having to meet strict environmental standards. But these levies also help prevent the export of hazardous industries to countries where regulation is lax. Such countries are in essence subsidizing domestic industries at the environment's expense, a practice that is coming to be known as "ecological dumping." But trade agreements have yet to recognize this concept. Instead, they tend to regard environmentally-motivated import tariffs as unfair trade barriers.[93]

The most logical solution to the trade and environment dilemma is to negotiate strict international environmental standards that require companies in every country to play by the same rules. This "level playing field" would insure both free trade and environmental protection in an increasingly global economy. But there are practical difficulties in negotiating a common policy. Forging a consensus among countries that have varied commitments to environmental protection and are at different stages of economic development is difficult. Some analysts fear that any achievable international standard would be a least common denominator that would eviscerate the environmental laws of more progressive countries.

Short of this, it might be possible to amend the GATT and other trade agreements to explicitly recognize that nations have the right to set their own domestic environmental laws, to clarify that trade sanctions have a legitimate role to play in environmental policymaking, and to permit import levies that discourage "ecological dumping". Since the tuna ruling, international environmental groups and the chairman of the U.S. Senate's International Trade Subcommittee, Max Baucus, have called for the negotiation of such an environmental code. Though this would satisfy most environmentalists, it would do little to address the concerns of those who worry that environmental policies are impeding free trade. Developing countries are particularly wary of barriers to their products that could be erected on pseudo-environmental grounds.[94]

In attempting to reconcile free trade and environmental goals, the European Community's experience merits attention. Like the GATT, the EC was originally founded to promote free trade. Unlike the GATT, however, the EC has changed with the times. It now has an extensive environmental policymaking function superimposed on its trade policies. Its rationale is that the only way to create a truly level playing field is to hold everyone to roughly the same rules. Since 1987, the EC has granted countries the right to exceed the EC's common standards if they like, so long as protecting the environment—rather than protecting domestic industries—is at the root of the stricter national legislation. In a landmark 1988 ruling, the European Court of Justice upheld the legitimacy of most aspects of a Danish returnable bottle program that everyone agreed had the effect of limiting free trade. The court reasoned that the Danish law's environmental benefits outweighed the constraint on commerce.[95]

Though it can be difficult to tell whether environmental or protectionist aims motivated a given policy, the EC's experience suggests that the tension between environmental and free trade goals can result in a ratcheting-up effect on environmental legislation among member countries, rather than the opposite. But devising a similar system for the GATT will prove trickier, given the fact that it has over 100 members as compared with the EC's 12, and that the GATT members are at widely differing stages of economic development and commitment to environmental protection. The more likely course is that regional trade agreements will continue to develop environmental overlays that are eventually replicated at the global level.[96]

The negotiations now under way for a U.S.-Mexico free trade agreement provide one such opportunity. Fearing that free trade considerations could require lowering U.S. environmental standards to Mexican levels, U.S. environmental groups and Congress pressured the Bush administration in May, 1991 to ensure that no U.S. environmental laws will be loosened. In addition, the administration agreed to develop a joint environmental plan with the Mexican government that will in theory strengthen standards and enforcement at Mexican plants just across the border, in order to discourage a boom in hazardous industries there. But a draft plan issued three months later proved weak on funding commitments and enforcement provisions, and the administration is under pressure to revise it.[97]

> "To developing countries, it often appears that the
> rich countries are hypocritically imposing
> environmental conditions on them while being
> unwilling to take action themselves."

The GATT itself is taking some halting steps toward grappling with the problem. A moribund working group on the relationship between trade and the environment, first established in the early seventies, has recently reconvened to discuss these difficult questions. But environmental groups fear the emphasis is mistakenly being placed on eliminating environmental policies that impede free trade, rather than vice-versa. Many developing countries, on the other hand, are strongly opposed to even discussing the connection between trade and the environment, given their worries that the industrialized world is using ecological concerns as an excuse to erect more barriers to their products.[98]

One troublesome aspect of the growing power of institutions such as the World Bank, the IMF, and trade agreements to affect environmental policy is the fact that the world's more powerful countries exert a disproportionate influence in these bodies. To developing countries, it often appears that the rich countries are hypocritically imposing environmental conditions on them while being unwilling to take actions themselves to solve problems such as global warming. One way to right this imbalance is to consider alternative schemes for distributing voting power in these bodies, as has been proposed for the Washington, D.C.-based Global Environment Facility. Opening these notoriously secretive international institutions to more extensive public participation would also help ease their inequitable distribution of power. Rather than rich countries manipulating the poor ones, world public opinion would be shaping governments.

Governing the Commons

As we approach the twenty-first century, the once-simple concept of national sovereignty has become increasingly frought with complications—and contradictions. On one level, nations are guarding their sovereignty more jealously than ever. The former Soviet Union has broken up into 15 independent nations, Yugoslavia has been wracked by gruesome civil warfare that could lead to its disintegration into as many as six more nations, and ethnic and tribal tensions are running rampant in many parts of the world.

At the same time, nations are finding that their interdependence is greater than ever before, with both the economy and the environment increasingly disrespectful of national borders. Thus, the European Community is becoming a dominant force in setting all manner of policies, and other regional organizations, such as the Association of Southeast Asian Nations, are beginning to follow its lead. Individual countries or groups of countries are also turning to the United Nations and the international economic institutions to regulate conduct between them. Jean Monnet, a founder of the EC, wrote in the 1950s, "Like our provinces in the past, our nations today must live together under common rules and institutions freely arrived at. The sovereign nations of the past can no longer solve the problems of the present: They cannot ensure their own progress or control their own future."[99]

In the environmental arena, the progress nations have made toward the common rules and institutions Monnet refers to offers some reason for optimism that international cooperation will become, increasingly, the rule rather than the exception. As a result of the world community's united effort to combat ozone depletion, and the willingness of the developed countries to provide financial and technical assistance, millions of lives will be saved. While progress on the climate change negotiations seems slow compared to the urgency of the problem, it has been rapid by historic standards of international diplomacy— particularly considering that a mere five years ago, most people around the world had never even heard of global warming.

Though they may be reluctant to admit it, time and time again over the past few decades nations have in effect ceded to international bodies the power to make decisions with large implications for domestic life. Gareth Porter and Janet Welsh Brown of the Washington-based Environmental and Energy Study Institute and World Resources Institute write: "On one issue after another, veto states have retreated in the face of new evidence of environmental threats and domestic and international pressures for change.... Something going beyond traditional power politics is clearly at work in global environmental politics." In effect, the whole notion of "national interest" needs to be reoriented from rivalry to cooperation.[100]

Though the progress to date offers reason for hope, the magnitude of the challenges facing the international community is still daunting. While diplomats debate, primary forests continue to be felled, irreplaceable genes disappear as species become extinct, and power plants and cars pump heat-trapping carbon dioxide into the atmosphere. What is being lost is not only a natural heritage, but the resources upon which future economic productivity depends. Even where the greatest progress has been made, in slowing our assault on the ozone layer, degradation will continue for decades to come—making it impossible even to enjoy a sunny day without fear or risk of contracting cancer. If the world had acted in the early seventies when scientists first theorized that human activities were damaging the ozone layer, this tragedy—perhaps the first to touch virtually every human on earth—could have been avoided.

Even in the best of circumstances, the slow pace of international diplomacy and the urgent rate at which the problems themselves are growing worse are difficult to reconcile. The best hope for speeding up the process of governing the global commons lies with the global citizenry. When governments act, it is generally in response to political pressure to do so. To some, the idea of global governance might seem hopelessly idealistic or quixotic; yet few would judge it any less conceivable than the astonishing events of the past two years in Eastern Europe and the former Soviet Union. These events demonstrated how quickly even the most seemingly-intransigent governments can be moved if their citizens feel passionate enough about their cause. When the cause is the air they breathe, the water they drink, and the climate that produces their food, the probability of an escalating pressure on their governments to take expeditious action is very real indeed.

A significant development is the growth of the international environmental movement. Friends of the Earth, Greenpeace, the World Wide Fund for Nature, and other organizations represent international constituencies rather than parochial national interests. Smaller, grassroots groups are springing up at a rapid pace in many parts of the world. Indigenous peoples who seek title to their lands are organizing as a political force. At the Earth Summit, the 20,000 concerned citizens and activists expected to attend from around the world may outnumber the official representatives by as much as two to one. As a next step, some have proposed the creation of an "Amnesty for the Earth" organization modeled after Amnesty International's pathbreaking work in the human rights field, that would investigate environmental violations and issue annual reports on states' environmental records. As environmentalists from around the world learn to work together for shared goals, the non-governmental movement stands to become as influential at the international level as it is within nations.[101]

For this to happen, however, the international governing process will need to be opened to public participation to a far greater extent than it is today. Presently, at the international level, there are no provisions for public review and comment, and no mechanisms for bringing citizen suits; nor is there anything resembling an elected parliament in the United Nations itself or any of its agencies. Most international organizations are closed off to public participation, and even access to documents of critical interest to the public is highly restricted. International laws and institutions have traditionally functioned as compacts between nations; but if they are to solve the problems of a rapidly deteriorating biosphere, they must also evolve into compacts between people.[102]

An equally large challenge for international governance is to be responsive to the entire global community, and not become a means by which the powerful countries of the world force their own agendas onto those with less economic clout and military might. The explosion of international diplomatic activity in this field has made it difficult for poor countries even to send qualified representatives to the numerous meetings on environmental issues now taking place around the world.[103]

Individual countries will not vigorously pursue—and may actively resist—the movement toward international governance unless they see that they have something to gain from it. For all countries, there is the ultimate benefit of staving off the kinds of climate change and pollution that could ruin crops or flood cities, or destroy resistance to disease. But for developing countries, this still will not be ample incentive, partly because for them, environmental problems are unsolvable without help from the richer countries, and partly because other problems are often more immediate. Any calls for strengthened global governance will continue to be viewed warily so long as industrial countries do not offer the things developing countries most urgently need: financial and technological assistance to combat environmental degradation directly, and help with structural economic problems such as debt and deteriorating terms of trade that exacerbate Third World poverty and in turn only

make the environmental problems worse. Combatting the losses of biological diversity and tropical forests, in particular, will require addressing the current inequities in the global economic system. Countries rich
in these resources will be unwilling to preserve them for the common
good unless the world community makes it in their interests to do so.

Global environmental governance may sound like a utopian concept.
But it is in fact well on the way to becoming a hard reality, as the worldwide shutting down of CFC production, for example, is showing. Far
from utopian, such governance is proving to be a practical and unavoid-
able response to otherwise-unmanageable threats. There can be little
doubt that as the international economy, the communications revolution, and the global environmental predicament all continue to make the
world more interdependent, nations will have to adapt more rapidly to
changing times.

To create an effective system of international environmental governance
will require wide departures from business as usual. But there is little
choice. The world faces a future of climbing global temperatures, depleted fisheries, reduced agricultural yields, diminished biological diversity,
and growing human suffering, unless governments move quickly. Only
by joining forces in forms of environmental governance that are stronger
than the sum of their parts, will nations be able to secure their citizens'
futures.

Notes

50

1. Shevardnadze's "day of Chernobyl" was the day complaints of spreading radiation began coming to his office; the actual date of the explosion was two days earlier, April 26. "USSR's Shevardnadze Views Ecology Impact on Soviet, World Politics," *Mezhdunarodnaya Zhizn*, Moscow, October 1990, translated in Foreign Broadcast Information Service (FBIS) Environmental Issues Report, Rosslyn, Va., January 4, 1991.

2. John Tagliabae, "Rhine Poisoning Stretching 185 Miles," *New York Times*, November 11, 1986; International Institute for Environment and Development and the World Resources Institute, *World Resources 1987* (New York: Basic Books, 1987); James Brooke, "Waste Dumpers Turning to West Africa," *New York Times*, July 17, 1991; "14,000 Barrels of Toxic Waste Returned to Italy After Illegal Dumping in Nigeria," *International Environment Reporter*, January 1989; photograph of Koko, Nigeria in Alfredo Jaar Exhibit, Anderson Gallery, Virginia Commonwealth University, Richmond, Virginia, Autumn 1991.

3. Number on shared river basins from United Nations Environment Programme (UNEP), "UNEP Profile," Nairobi, July 1990.

4. For a discussion of both the traditional and the evolving concepts of national sovereignty, see Gordon C. Schloming, *Power and Principle in International Affairs* (New York: Harcourt Brace Jovanovich, 1991) and Werner Levi, *Contemporary International Law* (Boulder, Colo.: Westview Press, 1991).

5. Description of Swiss diplomatic effort from Lynton K. Caldwell, "Beyond Environmental Diplomacy: The Changing Institutional Structure of International Cooperation," in John E. Carroll, ed., *International Environmental Diplomacy* (New York: Cambridge University Press, 1988); number of treaties from U.S. International Trade Commission (ITC), *International Agreements to Protect the Environment and Wildlife* (Washington, D.C.: 1991). See also, UNEP, *Register of International Treaties and Other Agreements in the Field of the Environment* (Nairobi: 1991). On the establishment of UNEP and the Stockholm Conference, see Peter S. Thacher, "Background to Institutional Options for Management of the Global Environment and Global Commons," a preliminary paper for the World Federation of United Nations Associations, project on Global Security and Risk Management, 1991.

6. Philip Shabecoff, "Suddenly, the World Itself Is a World Issue," *New York Times*, December 25, 1988; James Markham, "Paris Group Urges 'Decisive Action' for Environment," *New York Times*, July 17, 1989; Summit of the Arch, "Economic Declaration," Paris, July 16, 1989.

7. Debora MacKenzie, "Strong Words to Save the Planet," *New Scientist*, August 10, 1991; Maurice F. Strong, "Preparing for the UN Conference on Environment and Development," *Environment*, June 1991.

8. Maurice Strong, "Beyond Foreign Aid—Toward a New World System," presented to the International Development Conference, Washington, D.C., March 19, 1987; on the European Community's environmental policies, see Hilary F. French, "The EC—Environmental Proving Ground," *World Watch*, November-December 1991; on the Central American Commission on Environment and Development see "Central American

Agreement for the Protection of the Environment," San José, Costa Rica, December 11, 1989.

9. Alan B. Durning, *Poverty and the Environment: Reversing the Downward Spiral*, Worldwatch Paper 92 (Washington, D.C.: Worldwatch Institute, November 1989); *The Challenge to the South: The Report of the South Commission* (New York: Oxford University Press, 1990).

10. Emissions data from Trond Iverson et al., *Calculated Budgets for Airborne Acidifying Components in Europe, 1985, 1987, 1988, 1989, and 1990*, Technical Report No. 91 (Trondheim, Norway: Det Norske Meteorologiske Institutt, August, 1991), for the European Monitoring and Evaluation Program, U.N. Economic Commission for Europe, Geneva; chlorofluorocarbon consumption data a Du Pont 1992 estimate, from Mack McFarland, E.I. Du Pont Company, Wilmington, Del., private communication, February 7, 1992; William K. Stevens, "Ozone Loss Over the U.S. is Found to be Twice as Bad as Predicted," *New York Times*, April 5, 1991; International Physicians for the Prevention of Nuclear War and Institute for Energy and Environmental Research, *Radioactive Heaven and Earth* (New York: Apex Press, 1991); William Mahoney, "Most Mediterranean Beaches Safe, U.N. Environment Official Claims," *Multinational Environmental Outlook*, August 4, 1988; "Industrial, Agricultural Wastes Continue to Pose Threat to Mediterranean," *International Environmental Reporter*, May 9, 1990; Eugene H. Buck, "Whale Conservation," U.S. Congressional Research Service, August 30, 1990, Keith Schneider, "Iceland Plans to Withdraw from International Whaling Agreement," *New York Times*, December 28, 1991; Ronald Orenstein, "Africa's Elephants Could Soon Be Under the Gun Again," *Christian Science Monitor*, February 2, 1992; Lee A. Kimball, *Southern Exposure* (Washington, D.C.: World Resources Institute, November 1990); waste trade information from Heather Spalding, Greenpeace International, private communication, February 10, 1992, and from "Waste Traders Shift Focus to Latin America," *Greenpeace Waste Trade Update*, Summer, 1991.

11. Garrett Hardin, "The Tragedy of the Commons," *Science*, December 13, 1968.

12. James E. Hansen, Goddard Institute for Space Studies, National Aeronautics and Space Administration (NASA), "The Greenhouse Effect: Impacts on Current Global Temperature and Regional Heat Waves," Testimony before the Committee on Energy and Natural Resources, U.S. Senate, Washington, D.C., June 23, 1988; P.D. Jones, Climatic Research Institute, University of East Anglia, Norwich, U.K., "Testimony to the U.S. Senate on Global Temperatures," before the Commerce Committee, U.S. Senate, Washington, D.C., October 11, 1990; William K. Stevens, "Separate Studies Rank '90 as World's Warmest Year," *New York Times*, January 10, 1991; Richard A. Kerr, "1991: Warmth, Chill May Follow," *Science*, January 17, 1992.

13. Countries agreed in July 1985 to cut sulfur dioxide emissions or their transboundary flows by 30 percent from 1980 levels by 1993. A few years later, in November 1988, they agreed to freeze nitrogen oxides (NO_x) emissions at 1987 levels in 1994, as well as to conduct further discussions beginning in 1996 aimed at achieving reductions. Governments reached agreement on a third protocol, on volatile organic compounds (VOC), precursors to ground-level ozone pollution, in November 1991. This accord calls for a 30 percent reduction in VOC emissions from any year between 1984 and 1990, by 1999. UNEP, *Register of International Treaties*; "Emissions are falling...but is it enough?" *Acid Magazine*, September 1989; "25 ECE Members Sign Protocol to Limit Emissions of Nitrogen Oxides," *International Environment Reporter*, November 1988; "Nations Adopt Accord on Pollution Reduction," *Journal of Commerce*, November 19, 1991; Marc Levy, "European Acid Rain: The Power of Toteboard Diplomacy," draft paper prepared for the Harvard University Center for International Affairs, Project on International Environmental Institutions, November, 1991; "Panel to Propose Expanding Emission Cuts Required Under Two Air Pollution Treaties," *International Environment Reporter*, June 19, 1991.

14. Richard Elliot Benedick, *Ozone Diplomacy* (Cambridge, Mass.: Harvard University Press, 1991); "Montreal Protocol on Substances That Deplete the Ozone Layer, Final Act," UNEP, Nairobi, 1987; U.S. Environmental Protection Agency (EPA) estimate cited in John Gliedman, "The Ozone Follies: Is the Pact Too Little, Too Late?" *The Nation*, October 10, 1987.

15. Benedick, *Ozone Diplomacy*; Malcolm W. Browne, "93 Nations Agree to Ban Chemicals that Harm Ozone Layer," *New York Times*, June 30, 1990.

16. Benedick, *Ozone Diplomacy*.

17. "Ozone Loss Over the U.S. is Found to be Twice as Bad as Predicted"; Kathy Sawyer, "Ozone-Hole Conditions Spreading," *Washington Post*, February 4, 1992; Liz Cook, Friends of the Earth, Testimony before the Environmental Protection Subcommittee, Committee on Environment and Public Works, U.S. Senate, Washington, D.C., July 30, 1991; "Montreal Protocol Parties to Study Earlier Phase-out Date for CFCs, Halons," *International Environment Reporter*, July 3, 1991; Martha Hamilton, "The Costly Race to Replace CFCs," *Washington Post*, September 29, 1991.

18. Hansen, "The Greenhouse Effect"; Jones, "Testimony to the U.S. Senate on Global Temperatures"; Stevens, "Separate Studies Rank '90 as World's Warmest Year"; Kerr, "1991: Warmth"; on effects of global warming, see Second World Climate Conference, "Final Conference Statement, Scientific/Technical Sessions," Second World Climate Conference, Geneva, November 7, 1990; on sea-level rise, see Jodi L. Jacobson, "Holding Back the Sea," in Lester R. Brown, et al., *State of the World, 1990* (New York: W. W. Norton & Co., 1990) and Maumoon Abdul Gayoom, speech before the Forty-second Session of the U.N. General Assembly, New York, October 19, 1987.

19. Center for Global Change, College Park, MD, "International Negotiations on Climate Change," a briefing paper prepared for the Climate Action Network U.S., Washington, D.C., January 30, 1991.

20. Elisabeth Mann Borgese, "The Law of the Sea," *Scientific American*, March 1983; United Nations, *A Quiet Revolution: The United Nations Convention on the Law of the Sea* (New York: U.N. Department of Public Information, 1984); Douglas M. Johnston, "Marine Pollution Agreements: Successes and Problems," in Carroll, *International Environmental Diplomacy*; U.N. Office for Ocean Affairs and the Law of the Sea, "International Institutions and Legal Instruments," UNCED Research Paper No. 10, U.N. Conference on Environment and

Development (UNCED), July 1991; Council on Ocean Law, "Summary of LOS Convention Articles on Protection of the Marine Environment," Special Report, December 1991.

21. Borgese, "The Law of the Sea"; Ann L. Hollick, "Managing the Oceans," *The Wilson Quarterly*, Summer 1984.

22. Madeleine Cheslow, legal assistant, Treaty Section, Office of Legal Affairs, United Nations, New York, private communication, January 29, 1992; Miranda Wecker, Center for International Environmental Law (CIEL)-U.S., Washington, D.C., private communication, October 4, 1991; Council on Ocean Law, "The United States and the 1982 UN Convention on the Law of the Sea: A Synopsis of the Treaty and Its Expanded Role in the World Today," Washington, D.C., 1989; World Commission on Environment and Development, *Our Common Future* (New York: Oxford University Press, 1987).

23. UNEP, *UNEP profile*; David Edwards, "Review of the Status of Implementation and Development of Regional Arrangements on Cooperation in Combatting Marine Pollution," in Carroll, *International Environmental Diplomacy*; members of Mediterranean Plan from Lynton Keith Caldwell, *International Environmental Policy: Emergence and Dimensions* (Durham: Duke University Press, 1990). See also, Peter M. Haas, *Saving the Mediterranean: The Politics of International Environmental Cooperation* (New York: Columbia University Press, 1990).

24. Don Hinrichsen, *Our Common Seas: Coasts in Crisis* (London: Earthscan in association with UNEP, 1990).

25. Peter M. Haas, University of Massachusetts, "Protecting the Baltic and North Seas from Pollution: Amplifying Domestic Concern," draft paper prepared for the Harvard University Center for International Affairs, Project on International Environmental Institutions, November 1991.

26. Ludwik A. Teclaff, "Fiat or Custom: The Checkered Development of International Water Law," *Natural Resources Journal*, Winter 1991; 2,000 number from a U.N. Food and Agricultural Organization index cited in "Progress Report on Development of Legal Instruments for Transboundary Waters," UNCED Preparatory Committee, August 12-September 4, 1991.

27. Zambezi information from UNEP, "Safeguarding the World's Water," UNEP Environment Brief No. 6, undated.

28. "U.N. Group Completes Work on Treaty to Protect International Watercourses," *International Environment Reporter*, November 6, 1991.

29. UNEP, *Register of International Treaties*; Simone Bilderbeek, Wouter J. Veening, Ankie Wijgerde, Netherlands National Committee for the International Union for the Conservation of Nature, background document to the Global Consultation on the Development and Enforcement of International Environmental Law, with a Special Focus on the Preservation of Biodiversity, International Environmental Law Conference, The Hague, August 12-16, 1991.

30. UNEP, *Register of International Treaties*; ITC, *International Agreements*; Schneider, "Iceland Plans to Withdraw."

31. Biodiversity loss figure from Ariel E. Lugo, "Estimating Reductions in Diversity of Tropical Forest Species," in E.O. Wilson, ed., *Biodiversity* (Washington, D.C.: National Academy Press, 1988); "Biodiversity: A Progress Report on the Convention and the Strategy," *Global Environmental Change Report*, August 16, 1991.

32. "Biodiversity: A Progress Report"; Darrell Posey, "Effecting International Change," *Cultural Survival Quarterly*, Summer 1991; William Booth, "U.S. Drug Firm Signs Up to Farm Tropical Forests," *Washington Post*, September 21, 1991.

33. "New Deforestation Rate Figures Announced," *Tropical Forest Programme* (IUCN Newsletter), August 1990; Gareth Porter and Janet Brown, *Global Environmental Politics* (Boulder, Colorado: Westview Press, 1991); John Madeley, "Revamp Planned for Tropical Forest Body," *Financial Times*, March 27, 1991; "TFAP Progress Reported," *ISTF News*, December 1991; "PrepCom II: What Was Accomplished," *Earth Summit Update*, Environmental and Energy Study Institute (ESSI), Washington, D.C., July 1991; John Madeley, "Debt Problem Hampers Forestry Deal," *Financial Times*, August 21, 1991.

34. Stephen Kinzer, "Aiding Amazon Forest Gains Support in West," *New York Times*, November 7, 1991; Christina Lamb, "Talks Raise Hopes for Amazonian Rainforest Project," *Financial Times*, December 9, 1991; "Pilot Program to Conserve the Brazilian Rain Forest - Background Materials for the Press," Geneva, December 7, 1991.

35. The original twelve were Argentina, Australia, Belgium, Chile, France, Japan, New Zealand, Norway, South Africa, the United Kingdom, the United States, and the Soviet Union. Kimball, *Southern Exposure*.

36. "Protocol to Protect Antarctica Signed by 31 Nations at Meeting," *International Environment Reporter*, October 9, 1991; Alan Riding, "Pact Bans Oil Exploration in Antarctica," *New York Times*, October 5, 1991.

37. Kimball, *Southern Exposure*; current number of parties from Raymond Arnaudo, U.S. Department of State, private communication, February 5, 1992; World Commission on Environment and Development, *Our Common Future*.

38. Hilary F. French, "A Most Deadly Trade," *World Watch*, July-August 1990; Edward Cody, "Pact Seeks to Shield Third World States," *Washington Post*, March 23, 1989; Marguerite Cusack, "International Law and the Transboundary Shipment of Hazardous Waste to the Third World: Will the Basel Convention Make a Difference?" *The American University Journal of International Law and Policy*, Winter 1990; "System to Warn Nations of Banned Chemicals Close to Implementation, U.S. Official Says," *International Environment Reporter*, June 5, 1991.

39. Cusack, "International Law and the Transboundary Shipment of Hazardous Waste."

40. "Waste Shipments to 68 African, Caribbean and Pacific Countries will be Prohibited,"

Greenpeace Waste Trade Update, December 1989; "Africa Adopts Sweeping Measures to Protect Continent from Toxic Terrorism," *Greenpeace Waste Trade Update,* March 22, 1991. The total membership in the agreement with the EC is now 69, with Namibia having joined after attaining independence from South Africa.

41. Joseph LaDou, "Deadly Migration: Hazardous Industries' Flight to the Third World," *Technology Review,* July 1991; Barry Castleman, "Workplace Health Standards and Multinational Corporations in Developing Countries," in Charles S. Pearson, ed., *Multinational Corporations, Environment, and the Third World: Business Matters* (Durham, N.C.: Duke University Press in cooperation with World Resources Institute, 1987).

42. Peter S. Thacher, "Focussing on the Near Term: Alternative Legal and Institutional Approaches to Global Change," in World Resources Institute, *Greenhouse Warming: Negotiating a Global Regime* (Washington, D.C.: 1991); Peter H. Sand, *Lessons Learned in Global Environmental Governance* (Washington, D.C.: World Resources Institute, 1990).

43. Deposition imports calculated by Worldwatch Institute, based upon Iverson et al., *Calculated Budgets for Airborne Acidifying Components;* Lars Björkdom, "Resolution of Environmental Problems: the Use of Diplomacy," in Carroll, Ed., *International Environmental Diplomacy;* Benedick, *Ozone Diplomacy.*

44. James MacNeill, "The Meshing of the World's Economy and the Earth's Ecology," in Steve Lerner, *Earth Summit: Conversations with Architects of an Ecologically Sustainable Future* (Bolinas, Calif.: Common Knowledge Press, 1991); Donald M. Goldberg, "Procedures for Adopting and Amending Conventions and Protocols," CIEL-U.S., Washington, D.C., 1991.

45. Porter and Brown, *Global Environmental Politics;* Benedick, *Ozone Diplomacy;* Karen Schmidt, "Industrial Countries' Responses to Global Climate Change," *Environmental and Energy Study Institute Special Report,* Washington, D.C., July 1, 1991; Nigel Haigh, "The European Community and International Environmental Policy," Institute for European Environmental Policy, London, January 1991.

46. Benedick, *Ozone Diplomacy;* on Basel, Jane Bloom, formerly with the Natural Resources Defense Council, Remarks before Council on Foreign Relations discussion group on "Exporting Environmental Hazards: Whose Responsibility?," Washington, D.C., September 10, 1990; Porter and Brown, *Global Environmental Politics;* "PrepCom Opens its Process to Participation," *Network '92* (The Centre for Our Common Future, Geneva), October 1990; Victoria Dompka, "No Frivolity Please, We're British!," *ECO* (NGO Newsletter, Climate Change Negotiations, Nairobi), September 17, 1991.

47. Porter & Brown, *Global Environmental Politics.*

48. French, "A Most Deadly Trade"; Ron Scherer, "Support Grows to Protect Antarctic," *Christian Science Monitor,* April 17, 1991.

49. Porter and Brown, *Global Environmental Politics.*

50. Armin Rosencranz and Reina Milligan, "CFC Abatement: The Needs of Developing

Countries," *Ambio*, October 1990; Douglas G. Cogan, *Stones in a Glass House: CFCs and Ozone Depletion* (Washington, D.C.: Investor Responsibility Research Center, 1988); ozone fund commitments from Interim Multilateral Fund for the Implementation of the Montreal Protocol, Montreal, Que., Canada, private communication, February 4, 1992. For more information on the ozone fund, see Donald M. Goldberg, "Technological Cooperation and the Montreal Protocol Multilateral Fund: A Brief Description," CIEL-U.S., Washington, D.C., June 1991.

51. Eric Christensen and Samantha Geffin, "GATT Sets Its Nets on Environmental Regulation," *Inter-American Law Review*, forthcoming; "U.S. Bans Importing Fish Caught With Drift Nets," *Washington Post*, September 20, 1991; Tom Kenworthy, "Japan to End Drift Net Fishing in Bow to Worldwide Pressure," *Washington Post*, November 27, 1991; Donald M. Goldberg, CIEL-U.S.., "Provisions of the Montreal Protocol Affecting Trade," draft, January 16, 1992.

52. Benedick, *Ozone Diplomacy*; Goldberg, "Procedures for Adopting and Amending Conventions and Protocols"; Philip J. Hilts, "Senate Backs Faster Protection of Ozone Layer as Bush Relents," *New York Times*, February 7, 1992.

53. Sand, *Lessons Learned*; Lee A. Kimball, "International Law and Institutions: The Oceans and Beyond," *Ocean Development and International Law*, Vol. 20, 1989; Kimball, *Southern Exposure*; Porter and Brown, *Global Environmental Politics*; on the ILO, see James Avery Joyce, *World Labor Rights and Their Protection* (London: Croom Helm, 1980); "Survey of Existing International Agreements and Instruments and Its Follow Up," UNCED Preparatory Committee, March 2-April 3, 1992.

54. Abram Chayes and Antonia H. Chayes, "Adjustment and Compliance Processes in International Regulatory Regimes," in Jessica Tuchman Mathews, ed., *Preserving the Global Environment: The Challenge of Shared Leadership* (New York: W.W. Norton & Co., 1991); Geir Arne Bore, "Norge Bryter Miljø-Avtaler," *Bellona Magasin*, Nr.1, 1991.

55. Abram Chayes and Antonia Handler Chayes, "Compliance Without Enforcement: State Behavior Under Regulatory Treaties," *Negotiation Journal*, July 1991; Elizabeth P. Barratt-Brown, "Building a Monitoring and Compliance Regime Under the Montreal Protocol," *Yale Journal of International Law*, Vol. 16, No.2, 1991; Haas, "Protecting the Baltic and North Seas".

56. Benedick, *Ozone Diplomacy*; Porter and Brown, *Global Environmental Politics*; Kimball, *Southern Exposure*.

57. Scott Hajost and Quinlan J. Shea, "An Overview of Enforcement and Compliance Mechanisms in International Environmental Agreements," presented to International Enforcement Workshop, Utrecht, the Netherlands, May 8-10, 1990; Kimball, "International Law and Institutions"; Kimball, *Southern Exposure*.

58. Barratt-Brown, "Building a Monitoring and Compliance Regime"; John Simpson, "NPT Stronger after Iraq," *Bulletin of the Atomic Scientists*, October 1991; Chayes and Chayes, "Adjustment and Compliance Processes"; see also Owen Greene, University of

Bradford, "Building a Global Warming Convention: Lessons from the Arms Control Experience?" in "Pledge and Review Processes: Possible Components of a Climate Convention," Royal Institute of International Affairs, London, report of a workshop held August 2, 1991.

59. Alan Mager, U.S. National Marine Fisheries Service, Silver Spring, MD private communications, October 23, 1991 and February 4, 1992; "U.N. Urges Ban on Drift-Net Fishing By 1993," *Washington Post*, December 22, 1991.

60. "U.S. Imposes Ban on Imports of Endangered Animals, Goods," *Washington Post*, July 19, 1991; "International Ban Imposed on Thai Wildlife Trade," *The Nation*, Bangkok, April 16, 1991, translated in FBIS Environmental Issues Report, Rosslyn, Va., May 31, 1991; ITC, *International Agreements*; Kimball, "International Law and Institutions."

61. Goldberg, "Technological Cooperation and the Montreal Protocol Multilateral Fund"; "Little Progress Seen in Talks on Biological Diversity Convention," *International Environment Reporter*, October 9, 1991; "All Mouth, Too Little Money," *ECO* (NGO Newsletter, Climate Change Negotiations, Nairobi), September 16, 1991; "PrepCom Makes No Progress on Financial Resources," *Earth Summit Update* (EESI, Washington, D.C.), September 1991; Madeley, "Debt Problem Hampers Forestry Deal."

62. "Intellectual Property and Technology Transfer: An Uneasy Relationship," *Global Environmental Change Report*, September 28, 1990; "The Issue of Technology," *Network '92* (The Centre for Our Common Future, Geneva), August 1991; "Nordic Nations Offer Solution to Issue of Technology Transfer," *International Environment Reporter*, September 11, 1991.

63. Chayes and Chayes, "Adjustment and Compliance Processes."

64. U.S. General Accounting Office (GAO), *International Environment: International Agreements are Not Well Monitored* (Washington, D.C.: January, 1992); "President Bush's Fiscal 1993 Budget Proposal," *Environmental and Energy Study Institute Special Report*, Washington, D.C. January 30, 1992.

65. Hajost and Shea, "An Overview of Enforcement and Compliance Mechanisms."

66. Barratt-Brown, "Building a Monitoring and Compliance Regime"; Chayes and Chayes, "Adjustment and Compliance Processes"; GAO, "International Agreements."

67. Borgese, "The Law of the Sea"; Kimball, "International Law and Institutions"; Proposal Submitted by the PENTAGONALE countries and Poland, "Elements for a Resolution on Settlement of International Disputes Concerning the Environment," to UNCED Preparatory Committee, March 27, 1991.

68. Sir Geoffrey Palmer, former prime minister of New Zealand, "Toward a New International Law for the Environment" (draft), April 16, 1991; United Nations Association of the United States (UNA-USA) and the Sierra Club, *Uniting Nations for the Earth: An Environmental Agenda for the World Community* (New York: 1990); Pamela Leonard and

Walter Hoffman, *Effective Global Environmental Protection: World Federalist Proposals to Strengthen the Role of the United Nations* (Washington, D.C.: World Federalist Association, 1990); Philippe Sands, "The Environment, Community, and International Law," *Harvard International Law Journal*, Spring 1989; French, "The EC—Environmental Proving Ground."

58

69. David Reed, *The Global Environmental Facility: Sharing Responsibility for the Biosphere* (Washington, D.C.: World Wide Fund for Nature (WWF)-International, 1991); "First Round of Projects to be Funded Under Green Fund Announced by World Bank," *International Environment Reporter*, May 8, 1991; "The Global Environment Facility," *Our Planet* (UNEP), Vol. 3, No. 3, 1991; Frederik van Bolhuis, Global Environment Facility, Washington, D.C., private communication, November 5, 1991.

70. "Beijing Ministerial Declaration on Environment and Development," Ministerial Conference of Developing Countries on Environment and Development, Beijing, June 18-19, 1991; "Minister Vows to Vigorously Support Plan for a Third World `Green' Fund," *International Environment Reporter*, July 17, 1991; van Bolhuis, private communication, January 22, 1992; Valery Smirnov, Interim Multilateral Fund for the Implementation of the Montreal Protocol, Montreal, Quebec, Canada, private communication, February 10, 1992; "Global Environment Facility Remains an Empty Vessel," *ECO* (NGO Newsletter, Climate Change Negotiations), June 1991; "GEF Guidelines Criticized," *ECO*, September 18, 1991.

71. Bilderbeek et al., background document to the Global Consultation; "Survey of Existing International Agreements and Instruments" and "Institutional Proposals," UNCED Preparatory Committee, March 2 - April 3, 1992.

72. For summaries of various proposals, see Patricia A. Bliss-Guest, U.S. Council on Environmental Quality, "Proposals for Institutional Reform of the UN System to Promote Sustainable Development Policies," presented at Twentieth Annual American Bar Association Conference on the Environment, Warrenton, Va., May 18, 1991; "Progress Report on Institutions," UNCED Preparatory Committee, March 18-April 5, 1991, August 12-September 4, 1991, and March 2-April 3, 1992; U.N. Office of Public Information, *Charter of the United Nations and Statute of the International Court of Justice* (New York: United Nations); Robert E. Riggs and Jack C. Plano, *The United Nations: International Organization and World Politics* (Chicago: The Dorsey Press, 1988).

73. The Centre for Our Common Future, "Background information on the Hague Declaration," press release (includes a copy of the declaration from conference held March 10-11, 1989), Geneva, undated; Gro Harlem Brundtland, Prime Minister of Norway and Chairman of the World Commission on Environment and Development, "Global Change and Our Common Future," The Benjamin Franklin Lecture, National Academy of Sciences, Washington, D.C., May 2, 1989.

74. Sands, "The Environment, Community, and International Law"; Durwood Zaelke and James Cameron, CIEL-U.S., "Global Warming and Climate Change—An Overview of the International Legal Process," *The American University Journal of International Law and Policy*, Winter 1990; Palmer, "Toward a New International Law."

75. MacNeill, "The Greening of International Relations"; Porter and Brown, *Global*

Environmental Politics.

76. Bliss-Guest, "Institutional Reform of the UN System"; "Progress Report on Institutions."

77. "Statement by the U.S. Delegation on Institutional Issues," submitted to the third UNCED Preparatory Committee, Geneva, August 22, 1991; UNA-USA and the Sierra Club, *Uniting Nations for the Earth.*

78. Maurice Strong, "Statement" submitted to the UNCED Preparatory Committee, Geneva, April 2, 1991; UNEP, *UNEP Profile*; UNEP, "Proceedings of the Governing Council at its Sixteenth Session," Nairobi, June 30, 1991; "The National Wildlife Federation," information sheets, Washington, D.C., May 10, 1991; UNA-USA and Sierra Club, *Uniting Nations for the Earth*; Leonard and Hoffman, *Effective Global Environmental Protection.*

79. Bliss-Guest, "Proposals for Institutional Reform"; "Institutional Proposals," UNCED Preparatory Committee, March 2-April 3,1992; UNEP, *UNEP Profile*; UNEP, "Proceedings of the Governing Council at its Sixteenth Session"; "UNEP Governing Council Agrees to Expand Units Handling Industry, Environmental Law," *International Environment Reporter,* June 5, 1991.

80. "Report of the Aspen Institute Working Group on International Environment and Development Policy," Aspen, Colo., July 25, 1991; "Institutional Proposals, UNCED Preparatory Committee, March 2-April 3, 1992 .

81. The Stockholm Initiative on Global Security and Governance, "Common Responsibility in the 1990s," Prime Minister's Office, Stockholm, April 22, 1991; Lucia Mouat, "Global Commission Urges Reform of United Nations," *Christian Science Monitor,* May 30, 1991.

82. Stockholm Initiative, "Common Responsibility in the 1990s"; Bliss-Guest, "Proposals for Institutional Reform"; Mouat, "Global Commission Urges Reform"; Gerry Gray, "Italy Urges Sweeping Structural Changes at U.N.," *New York Times,* September 28, 1991; see also Helena Cobban, "Let's Rethink the Security Council," *Christian Science Monitor,* July 9, 1991.

83. Bliss-Guest, "Proposals for Institutional Reform"; Mouat, "Global Commission Urges Reform."

84. Raymond F. Mikesell & Lawrence F. Williams, *International Banks and the Environment: From Growth to Sustainability—An Unfinished Agenda* (San Francisco: Sierra Club Books, forthcoming, April 1992); Barber B. Conable, President, World Bank, "The World Bank and International Finance Corporation," presented to the World Resources Institute, Washington, D.C. May 5, 1987; lending program for 1991, from World Bank, *The World Bank Annual Report 1991* (Washington, D.C.: 1991); World Bank, *The World Bank and the Environment: A Progress Report* (Washington, D.C.: 1991); "World Bank Says Its Loans Reflect Growing Environmental Sensitivity," *International Environment Reporter,* October 23, 1991. The accounting system used in previous years did not identify environmental projects as such, so the $400 million is approximate, according to Getachew Abdi, World Bank, private communication, January 29, 1992.

85. "World Bank Says its Loans Reflect Growing Environmental Sensitivity"; Sandra Postel and Christopher Flavin, "Reshaping the Global Economy," in Lester R. Brown et al., *State of the World 1991* (New York: W.W. Norton & Co., 1991); employees and offices from World Bank, *Annual Report 1991*; Bruce Rich, "The Emperor's New Clothes: The World Bank and Environmental Reform," *World Policy Journal,* Spring 1990.

86. The World Bank also devotes a considerable and growing portion of its funds to structural adjustment lending. The question of how to integrate environmental considerations into this type of lending is thus applicable to both World Bank and International Monetary Fund (IMF) programs. "The IMF and the World Bank," *The Economist,* October 12, 1991; IMF, *The IMF Annual Report 1991* (Washington, D.C.: 1991); Frances Stewart, "Back to Keynesianism: Reforming the IMF," *World Policy Journal,* Summer 1987.

87. Mikesell & Williams, *International Banks and the Environment;* "The IMF and the World Bank."

88. Marijke Torfs and Jim Barnes, Friends of the Earth, unpublished memorandum, September 4, 1991; Durning, *Poverty and the Environment.*

89. Mikesell & Williams, *International Banks and the Environment.*

90. Torfs and Barnes, unpublished memorandum.

91. General Agreement on Tariffs and Trade (GATT), "United States— Restrictions on Imports of Tuna: Report of the Panel," Geneva, September 3, 1991; Keith Bradsher, "U.S. Ban on Mexico Tuna is Overruled," *New York Times,* August 23, 1991; Hilary F. French, "GATT and the Environment: the Tuna Test," *World Watch,* March-April 1992.

92. Charles Arden-Clarke, *The General Agreement on Tariffs and Trade, Environmental Protection and Sustainable Development* (Gland, Switzerland: WWF-International, 1991); Francois Nectoux and Yoichi Kuroda, *Timber from the South Seas: An Analysis of Japan's Tropical Timber Trade and its Environmental Impact* (Gland, Switzerland: WWF-International, April 1989).

93. Arden-Clarke, *The General Agreement on Tariffs and Trade.*

94. Statement of Senator Max Baucus, Chairman, International Trade Subcommittee, U.S. Senate Finance Committee, "Trade and the Environment," September 17, 1991; John Zarocosta, "Group Appeals to UN for Global Ecology Code," *Journal of Commerce,* September 5, 1991; C. Raghavan, "Third World Cool to GATT Role in Environment," *Third World Economics,* March 1-15, 1991.

95. French, "The EC—Environmental Proving Ground"; *Environmental Policy in the European Community, Fourth Edition* (Luxembourg: Office for Official Publications of the European Communities, 1990); "Landmark EEC Court Case on Returnable Bottles Gives

Boost to Environment," *Ends Report*, September 1988; "Commission of the European Communities v. Kingdom of Denmark - Case 302/86," *Report of Cases Before the Court, Vol. 8* (Luxembourg: Office for Official Publications of the European Communities, 1988). The ruling was not a complete victory for the environment, as one element of the Danish law requiring that bottles be government-approved was overthrown by the Court as being "disproportionate" to the desired end. There had been some concern that this provision might reduce the number of returned bottles that are actually refilled rather than merely recycled, but this does not appear to have happened to any appreciable degree.

61

96. French, "The EC—Environmental Proving Ground"; C. Raghavan, "North-South Divide Over GATT Involvement in Environment," *Third World Economics*, April 1- 15, 1991; Information and Media Relations, "General Agreement on Tariffs and Trade (GATT): What it Is, What it Does," GATT, Geneva, 1990.

97. John Maggs, "U.S. to Offer Environment Plan with Mexico Pact," *Journal of Commerce*, April 30, 1991; U.S. Environmental Protection Agency and Secretaria de Desarrollo Urbano y Ecología, "Integrated Environmental Plan for the Mexico-U.S. Border Area (First Stage, 1992-1994)," Working Draft, Washington, D.C., and Mexico City, August 1, 1991; Keith Bradsher, "U.S. and Mexico Draft Plan to Fight Pollution," *New York Times*, August 2, 1991; "Environmental Enforcement Provisions Must be Set Out in Trade Accord, U.S. Told," *International Environment Reporter*, October 9, 1991.

98. "Gatt Revives its Working Group on Environment," *Financial Times*, October 9, 1991; Justin R. Ward, Natural Resources Defense Council, private communication, November 25, 1991; Raghavan, "Third World Cool to GATT Role in Environment"; C. Raghavan, "North-South Divide Over GATT Involvement."

99. Philip Shenon, "Southeast Asia Nations Sign Free-Trade Accord," *New York Times*, January 29, 1992; Monnet cited in Jessica Mathews, "Giving Way to Global Concerns," *Washington Post*, August 22, 1991.

100. Porter and Brown, *Global Environmental Politics*.

101. Porter and Brown, *Global Environmental Politics*; Alan B. Durning, *Action at the Grassroots: Fighting Poverty and Environmental Decline*, Worldwatch Paper 88 (Washington, D.C.: Worldwatch Institute, January 1989); "'Forest Citizens' Want to Be Heard," *Christian Science Monitor*, October 24, 1991; Lester R. Brown et al., *State of the World 1992* (New York: W. W. Norton & Co., 1992); G.M. Oza, "Need for Amnesty for the Earth," *Environmental Awareness*, Vol. 14, No.2, 1991.

102. Sands, "The Environment, Community, and International Law"; Liz Barratt- Brown, Natural Resources Defense Council, "Working Paper on Reform of Global Environmental Institutions," prepared for Consortium for Action to Protect the Earth, Washington, D.C., June 10, 1991; David A. Wirth, Washington and Lee University School of Law, Remarks to National Association of Environmental Law Societies Conference, Washington, D.C., February 1, 1991.

103. "Survey of Existing International Agreements and Instruments."

62

HILARY F. FRENCH is a Senior Researcher at the Worldwatch Institute, where she researches international environmental politics. She is author of Worldwatch Paper 99, *Green Revolutions: Environmental Reconstruction in Eastern Europe and the Soviet Union*, Worldwatch Paper 94, *Clearing the Air: A Global Agenda*, and coauthor of three of the Institute's annual *State of the World* reports. She is a graduate of Dartmouth College, where she studied history.

THE WORLDWATCH PAPER SERIES

No. of
Copies

_____ 57. **Nuclear Power: The Market Test** by Christopher Flavin.
_____ 58. **Air Pollution, Acid Rain, and the Future of Forests** by
Sandra Postel.
_____ 60. **Soil Erosion: Quiet Crisis in the World Economy** by Lester R. Brown
and Edward C. Wolf.
_____ 61. **Electricity's Future: The Shift to Efficiency and Small-Scale Power**
by Christopher Flavin.
_____ 62. **Water: Rethinking Management in an Age of Scarcity** by
Sandra Postel.
_____ 63. **Energy Productivity: Key to Environmental Protection and
Economic Progress** by William U. Chandler.
_____ 65. **Reversing Africa's Decline** by Lester R. Brown and Edward C. Wolf.
_____ 66. **World Oil: Coping With the Dangers of Success** by
Christopher Flavin.
_____ 67. **Conserving Water: The Untapped Alternative** by Sandra Postel.
_____ 68. **Banishing Tobacco** by William U. Chandler.
_____ 69. **Decommissioning: Nuclear Power's Missing Link** by
Cynthia Pollock.
_____ 70. **Electricity For A Developing World: New Directions** by
Christopher Flavin.
_____ 71. **Altering the Earth's Chemistry: Assessing the Risks** by
Sandra Postel.
_____ 73. **Beyond the Green Revolution: New Approaches for Third World
Agriculture** by Edward C. Wolf.
_____ 74. **Our Demographically Divided World** by Lester R. Brown and Jodi L.
Jacobson.
_____ 75. **Reassessing Nuclear Power: The Fallout From Chernobyl** by
Christopher Flavin.
_____ 76. **Mining Urban Wastes: The Potential for Recycling** by
Cynthia Pollock.
_____ 77. **The Future of Urbanization: Facing the Ecological and Economic
Constraints** by Lester R. Brown and Jodi L. Jacobson.
_____ 78. **On the Brink of Extinction: Conserving The Diversity of Life** by
Edward C. Wolf.
_____ 79. **Defusing the Toxics Threat: Controlling Pesticides and Industrial
Waste** by Sandra Postel.
_____ 80. **Planning the Global Family** by Jodi L. Jacobson.
_____ 81. **Renewable Energy: Today's Contribution, Tomorrow's Promise** by
Cynthia Pollock Shea.
_____ 82. **Building on Success: The Age of Energy Efficiency** by Christopher
Flavin and Alan B. Durning.
_____ 83. **Reforesting the Earth** by Sandra Postel and Lori Heise.
_____ 84. **Rethinking the Role of the Automobile** by Michael Renner.
_____ 85. **The Changing World Food Prospect: The Nineties and Beyond** by
Lester R. Brown.
_____ 86. **Environmental Refugees: A Yardstick of Habitability** by
Jodi L. Jacobson.
_____ 87. **Protecting Life on Earth: Steps to Save the Ozone Layer** by
Cynthia Pollock Shea.
_____ 88. **Action at the Grassroots: Fighting Poverty and Environmental
Decline** by Alan B. Durning.
_____ 89. **National Security: The Economic and Environmental Dimensions**
by Michael Renner.
_____ 90. **The Bicycle: Vehicle for a Small Planet** by Marcia D. Lowe.

_____ **Total Copies**

☐ **Single Copy: $5.00**
☐ **Bulk Copies (any combination of titles)**
  ☐ 2–5: $4.00 each   ☐ 6–20: $3.00 each   ☐ 21 or more: $2.00 each

☐ **Membership in the Worldwatch Library: $25.00 (overseas airmail $40.00)**
The paperback edition of our 250- page "annual physical of the planet,"
State of the World 1992, plus all Worldwatch Papers released during
the calendar year.

☐ **Subscription to *World Watch* Magazine: $15.00 (overseas airmail $30.00)**
Stay abreast of global environmental trends and issues with our award-winning,
eminently readable bimonthly magazine.

No postage required on prepaid orders. Minimum $3 postage and handling
charge on unpaid orders.

Make check payable to Worldwatch Institute
1776 Massachusetts Avenue, N.W., Washington, D.C. 20036-1904 USA

Enclosed is my check for U.S. $_____

_____

name   **daytime phone #**

_____

address

_____

city   **state**   **zip/country**